Musings on Death and Dying

- a collection of short stories about a topic that touches all of us.

Esther Jacoby

In loving memory of F.

Thanks for the inspiration, kiddo, but I'd rather you still were here!

Back cover art by Laith Al-Musawi:

Thanks for the inspiring cooperation. May your dreams come true and one day the right people discover you!

Content

The Meltdown

The mobile phone vibrated on the polished kitchen table and danced to its own impulses.

Tina knew who was calling; she had expected this call, and yet it took six or seven rings for her to bring up the energy to slide her finger across the smooth display and start the conversation.

'Hello?' she asked into the smoothness of the interface, for no other reason than this was the way she always answered phone calls.

'Hi darling', Henry's voice sounded clear and near, like a fresh summer wind, like white curtains billowing in a breeze by an open balcony door.

'How are you? What took you so long? Have you been napping?'

Her husband called from the other side of the globe and yet there seemed to be not even a mini-second of a delay in the line. The marvels of technology!

'No, I have been right here. But have you seen the news? This weekend is the hottest weekend in the UAE since they started recording temperatures. It is sooooo hot, I don't want to move!'

Outside the circle of the AC high up on the kitchen wall, sweat started to form on Tina's back. It pooled along her spine. She could feel the droplets forming at the back of her knees and in the crack of her butt. Uncomfortable, she wiped herself with a t-shirt from the pile of dirty clothes ready to be washed.

'Is it that hot? Then I am glad I am missing this weekend. Here, it is nice and cool. Why don't you up the AC?'

'I have done that already. All the ACs are on, in all the rooms, on the highest setting. But they are either too old, or just not built to deal with these kinds of temperatures! The moment I step away from their air stream, I start sweating and I end up looking like I just stepped out of the shower!'

Henry apologised for her situation, but in his tone, she could hear that he was glad to be far away. They briefly told of how much they missed each other, before he reminded her of his return on Sunday morning.

'Will you be there?' He asked. 'I think it will be around ten or 11 before I get in from Dubai.'

'I have the day off, and don't see why I should not be here. If I have to go to the office, I will leave a note for you.'

'Okay, hon, I miss you. Take it easy, okay?'

'I miss you, too.'

He disconnected first.

The phone had become hot and heavy in her hand. Where it touched her ear, her skin felt like it almost burnt.

Too hot, much too hot! To recover a little bit, she decided to lie on the bed, under the AC, and wait to see if she would stop sweating.

Out of the corner of her eyes she noticed some visual disturbance around the edges of her image as she passed the hall mirror.

'I need to start wearing my glasses, even indoors', she told herself as she slumped onto the shiny cotton sheets, she had picked only a few days ago. The old ones were entirely too soft and warm.

Above her, the AC blew cold air on the highest setting, gently caressing her up and down her naked body, lulling her slowly into a nap from which she woke sometime later. The gentle caress had turned into a choleric cough. Unbelieving, she stared in horror as the AC vomited out some humid, condensated air at the bed on which she lay, before it hiccupped one last time and died.

Tina rubbed her eyes and decided to call the landlord to report the need for most urgent repairs. She only hoped that there would be people available immediately to come and do the work. Or maybe she should simply go to get a new unit and demand reimbursement. Hmh. What to do?

Unseeing, still a little perturbed, she stumbled into her master bathroom for urgent relief.

She hit the flush and turned.

In the mirror, she hardly recognised herself. The person looking back was definitely her, but she seemed to have lost her distinctness of outline. The person looking back at her had somehow lost her sharpness.

Tina wiped her eyes and looked again, convincing herself that all was as it should be.

When she called the landlord, he did not pick up.

It was almost 4pm, the temperature had climbed to just over 50C, and Tina decided to get dressed to go to the mall to buy a new air conditioning unit for her bedroom to replace the one that had just died.

With even this one old AC out of action, the temperature in the apartment had risen already. Yes, she could sleep on the settee in the lounge, but that would kink her back and shoulders and it would be exceedingly uncomfortable, so she dismissed the idea. No, better to go and buy a new one. One that had more power.

In the bedroom, Tina angled a pair of shorts from her wardrobe. She noticed that her legs somehow had lost shape. Where they had been solid and defined before, they seemed to have turned soft and wobbly.

'I am losing my mind! This heat is getting to me!'

In the kitchen, she poured some tepid water from the weekly gallon bottle into a glass and thirstily drank it down, then a second. Before she could decide whether she had enough, her phone started vibrating on the kitchen table again.

'Hello?'

'I had a missed call from you?'

The Landlord.

Yes, indeed. I just wanted to let you know that the AC in my bedroom has given up. I was about to leave and buy a new unit ...'

'No need, no need', the man interrupted. 'I will bring a new unit. Just wait.'

'When will you come?' He had made empty promises before, so Tina was loathed to put her trust in him.

'I will be there in one hour. One hour, just wait!'

It was 4:30 now. One hour would make it 5:30. Even if he was late, there still would be enough time to install a new unit in her bedroom so she could sleep there that night. She agreed to wait.

In the meantime, Tina busied herself with small chores – housekeeping items that did not require too much movement.

When she passed the hall mirror again and thought that she was getting fuzzy round the edges, she went in search for her glasses. Resolutely, she pushed them onto her nose. But Tina's skin was so slippery with all the sweat that they kept falling down and in disgust with the entire situation, she flung them onto the polished kitchen table, where they came to rest next to her phone.

The afternoon turned into late afternoon turned into evening and still, the landlord did not show.

Around 8pm, she tried to call him again but received no reply.

Around 9pm, covered in sweat, Tina decided to sleep in the lounge where the AC at least was ineffectively blowing cool air and she did not feel too bad.

Around midnight, Tina rolled off the couch and wobbled on unsteady legs into her bedroom. The sofa was so uncomfortable that she might as well not sleep from heat but at least have her body supported by a sturdy mattress.

She lay in the darkness, wondering how she would be able to cope once Henry was back and the heat off his body would make both of them suffer. She lifted her arm to receive some cooling. Her skin shimmered moist. She raised first one leg, then the other, but there was no relief. In the end, Tina gave up and rolled from one sweaty patch on the bed to the next, hoping for the night to end.

On Saturday, the landlord stopped by to bring the promised new AC unit but when he rang their doorbell, nobody opened. He waited, he knocked just in case, and then simply went home: it was too hot to hang about and wait. One of them would call, no doubt, to remind him and then they would set up a time that suited all parties. He did not mind that they lost that AC in the bedroom: his AC units all worked.

When Henry called during a stopover in London, Tina did not answer the phone. She must be out, probably doing the shopping for his return. And he knew his wife:

she never answered her phone when she was out and about.

It was shortly after 10 on Sunday morning when Henry unlocked the door to his apartment.

'Tina, honey, I am home!'

He pushed his case into the hallway, waiting to hear Tina answer.

In the stillness of the dim, unlit hallway, he paused. Then he walked into the kitchen. Her phone and glasses lay on the kitchen table. He opened the fridge. The usual food stuffs were there, so Tina was not still out shopping. She was only gone a moment.

In the lounge, there was no note for him, but maybe she had to pop out to the office after all and simply forgot ... no, Tina would not forget!

'Tina?'

He kept calling her name, nonplussed. The AC units were on in all the rooms, as she had told him, they were all toiling away on the highest setting with little effect. The heat was stifling, but Henry was glad to be back nonetheless. But where was Tina? He shrugged and unpacked his suitcase in the kitchen where he dumped the dirty laundry in front of the washing machine.

Musing over Tina's absence, he wandered into the bedroom.

This was the only AC unit that was out of service. He remembered that in the past, this one had given them bother and he was not surprised.

There were new bedsheets, bright pink ones. They looked nice and cool. However, there were sweaty, greasy smudges all over. Clumps of hair lay curled in places. What had she done? Poor thing must have sweated so badly! Even now, the moisture had not dried. And her hair ... she always moulted in the summer, like a puppy dog ...

'I know what I will do!' He smiled to himself as he tore off the new sheets, rolled them up in his arms and carried them to the kitchen. Her essence had soaked so deeply into the material that he could smell her as if she was right there. He took a deep sniff and closed his eyes.

He pushed the soiled sheets into the washing machine, added some of his dirty shirts, powder and selected the super clean option. Tina would be pleased that he showed initiative.

He watched for a moment as water filled the round sight glass and the laundry started to tumble around and around inside the machine.

The Kattel

Three of them. Three little girls, borne within twelve months of each other. And even before they were old enough to care about social standing, they were well matched, so their elders let them be.

The oldest was Nelly: Borne in 1923 and growing up around three older brothers, she was boisterous and loud, not shy at all. Her hair was brown and scraggly. In the mornings, her mother tried to tame it into pigtails, but by lunchtime, there were tufts standing off in all directions. Nelly just laughed about it, shrugged it off, knowing in her heart of hearts that her hair never would win her prices but that she would do alright eventually as the daughter of a wealthy-enough farming family.

Almost her exact opposite and the youngest of the threesome was little Evi, the mayor's shy oldest child who had the fine hair of a baby, almost white, but who so much wanted to be dark haired that she was convinced that at the back of her head, her hair was as black as that of the fairy princess in the stories her Grandmother told her.

But the prettiest of them was little Kattel. She was the miller's daughter. Her hair was thick and the delicious colour of the loafs her father baked in the ovens out back. The heavy pleat of it hung way down her back, thick as a man's arm, and when she ran, her hair developed a rhythm of its own. Those running next to her had to avoid getting too close to her for fear of being sucker-punched by it. An only child, precocious and precious, she was easily influenced by Nelly and when Evi came around with her quiet nature, the characters of the three balanced well.

They knew each other from their first memory. Possibly, their mothers patted each other's pregnant bellies and then had them sat next to each other on their blankets when the grown-ups attended to the field work and babies and toddlers could not be left home alone. They grew up like the Princesses they were, playing, running free while they could. Before long, all three were expected to help their parents on their farms, their fields or their homes. All little girls grew up to be good helpers till their fathers found them husbands and turned them into good wives.

Evi was five, Nelly was already six, and Kattel was somewhere in-between. It was a nice day, and the girls had ambled their way down to the Ukrina to cool their feet in the fresh water. They played in the shallows, pushed sticks in the mud and tried to stay out of the way of the boys that were guarding the cows a little way up the river. Those boys would tease them and pull their pig tales if they caught them, so they kept a low profile, chatted, laughed, whispered about all those things that little girls whisper about. It was 1929, and world economics did not matter to them: their world was safe and they had all they could ever want. Most importantly, they had each other.

The afternoon progressed, and their little hands and feet got cold, their dresses wet and dirty, giving their mothers reasons to scold them later.

Nelly, always the driving force, eventually nudged the others out.

'Aren't you hungry? I am hungry', she stressed, rubbing her stomach to demonstrate her need.

Evi smoothed down her dress.

'Mammi will be angry. She only just washed this dress.'

Pushing her hands away so Evi could not rub the dirt deeper into the fabric, Nelly shook her head.

'By the time we get you home, it all will be dry, and you can just brush it off. You will see there will be no dirt left.'

Kattel simply laughed, the sound sparkling crystal clear in the shade under the trees. Nobody would reprimand her, no matter what state she came back home in.

Slowly, the girls made their way uphill to the village. Soon, the first houses greeted them.

Encouraged by the growling of Nelly's stomach, she nettled them to speed up. Her parents' house was the furthest away, but Kattel had an idea.

'It is Wednesday. Today, the wife of Farmer Michels is using the ovens. She always bakes extra. And she never guards the ovens, so we can take a loaf, she will not mind!'

'Are you sure?' Nelly's eyes lit up. Fresh bread ... yes, that would taste well right now! And Kattel's house was not that far off, they would get there it long before she reached her own home where nothing special was waiting for her. Fresh bread ... her mouth already could taste it; her teeth could already feel the crunch of it.

'Evi? Why are you looking so glum?'

Evi was hanging back, still upset about the mud on her pretty dress.

'I want to go to Grandma. I am sure she can help me clean this up!'

'But Kattel says there is fresh bread!'

Sad and distracted, Evi shook her head.

'I am not hungry. I want to see Grandma. Before Mammi finds out where we have been. And how dirty I am.'

Kattel shrugged.

'Well, we will see you tomorrow', she said as they hugged, Evi turning in one direction while the other two linked their arms and skip-hopped the other way.

They approached the miller's yard from the back so that the Michels woman and Kattel's mother would not notice them. They could have asked for fresh bread and would not have been denied it but opening the oven and taking some secretly was so grown up, they did not think twice.

They danced across the small creek that formed the border of the miller's property. The aroma of the bread in the ovens welcomed them. The girls exchanged smiles.

'I know how to do this, I watched my Mummy do it', said Kattel as she grabbed one of the peels leaning alongside. Carefully, she opened the oven. The roar of the fire and the crackling of the wood sounded loud and Kattel threw a worried glance towards the backdoor of their house.

Now that she was doing this, she was suddenly worried what her mother would say if she discovered her. Kattel was not allowed near the ovens on baking days. But no adults came running, and she leaned closer to reach one of the small breads that were almost ready. They had timed their arrival well.

Nelly stood by, watching, rubbing her anticipating stomach.

Later, she could not tell what exactly and how it happened.

Maybe, Kattel came too close, maybe a spark got blown up and out.

Kattel's hair was on fire.

Nelly shrieked.

'Kattel, the creek, jump!' she yelled, pulling her friend the few steps to the saving water. She was sure to have the younger girl by her sleeve as she herself rolled and splashed into the small stream.

As if she was rooted to the ground, Kattel had not moved.

Nelly's yelling had brought the women from the miller's kitchen.

Kattel's mother, seeing her only child aflame by the open door of the oven, started running and screaming for help, with the wife of Farmer Michels right behind her and others rushing in as fast as they could.

In the ensuing mayhem, someone grabbed Nelly and pulled her splashing and flailing out of the water.

Within hours, Nelly developed a fever. The only doctor was three days' travel away and could not be called, so the old women looked after her, boiled tea and sat with her, stroking her hands, her face. Hushed voices wove a background to Nelly's hallucinations and the nightmares that made her shriek and cry.

When she came to, Evi was sitting with her, smiling shyly.

'Kattel?'

Evi shook her head. Tears started and she swiped at them almost angrily. Had her mother not told her that Kattel had gone to a better place, that she was now an angel and with the Lord Jesus in heaven? Why should she cry? But cry she did. And when Nelly understood, she started crying, too. The girls huddled on the hard bed and cried in unison, like only best-friend little girls could do.

The next day, when Nelly was feeling better, she asked to see Kattel. Her mother told her no, but Nelly insisted.

The miller's daughter was laid out in a small room at the back of their house, waiting for the priest to return from his trip to some other villages he cared for. Messages had gone out for him to return, but there had not been word of him yet.

The grownups had said their goodbyes to the little girl whose beautiful hair now was a blackened, mangled and horrific mess. The old women had tried hard to cover the stench of burnt hair and flesh with offerings of fresh herbs and spices. Flowers were brought daily for the girl that waited to be buried.

Nelly had seen the flames leech off Kattel's head, had seen the first licks of flame catch her friend's clothes.

Now here lay pretty little Kattel, who would laugh and sing no more.

As Nelly studied her friend's disfigured body intently, Kattel opened her eyes. From bulging eyes whose lids had been burnt away, she looked directly at her friend. She moaned, her spoiled lips trying to form words.

Nelly shrieked.

'She is alive! Kattel is alive!'

A woman came running.

'Quiet, child.'

'No, honest, Kattel looked at me. She is alive!'

They dragged her away, kicking and screaming.

Nelly told Evi who told her father, the most important man in the village: Kattel is alive, their friend is not dead! But nobody listened.

'Hush, child', they were told. 'Kattel is dead. She burnt, trying to steal bread from the oven.' What happened to little Kattel would be made into a lesson for children to behave and pay obedience to their elders.

Nelly was put back to bed. She was forced to rest. She was not allowed to visit Kattel again; neither was Evi allowed to go to the miller's house.

Three days later, the priest returned, and a funeral was hurriedly arranged.

The procession wound its way from the miller's house to the church and the cemetery beyond.

Nelly was meant to stay in bed, but when her Greatgrandmother fell asleep by her side, she took her chance and escaped. She could not help herself, she had to see it. Hiding amongst the legs and coats of the adults along the way, she followed the coffin.

She could have sworn that she heard small fingers scratching the rough-hewn wood of the coffin.

Kattel was alive. Nelly knew it.

Kept

I have to leave in ten minutes', she whined.

'No problem', he replied with a smile.

Every day it was the same. On office mornings, she had a plan that made them get up two hours before either one of them had to leave the apartment just so all the usual routines were followed. On days like today, a rare, shared day off, her scheduling was almost unbearable. Harmony's running countdown of the remaining time before they had to be out of the door rang like a chime down his spine. The tinkle of her voice slowed him the more she tried to push.

'Eight minutes and you are still not dressed. Where is your shirt?'

Horace grabbed the only white shirt that was washed and held it for her to see.

'Can you please iron this for me?'

'You are joking, right? Why can you never be organised?'

Huffing and with her face turning red, the anger seething just below her pale skin, she wrangled the ironing board from its hiding place at the end of the kitchen counter. A practiced grip released its legs to their full extension. She flung it over, rattled it close to the power outlet at the far wall.

Helpfully, Horace took the iron from its box on the lowest shelf, plugged it in and laid the heating iron on the board.

'I should let you do the ironing, really! You should have told me last night or earlier this morning. Really!'

From the tone of her voice he understood that her anger was abating, and that Harmony was simply stressed. She did not want to be late and he felt for her.

While Harmony got busy on his shirt, Horace took out the trash.

'How much time?' he asked as he stepped back into the small kitchen.

Harmony was just finishing off the collar.

Without looking at him, focusing instead on the cotton material and the iron she held to it, she ignored him.

His eyes clung to her and the moment she finished her chore, she handed him the warm shirt.

'5. Don't you have a watch you could check? Why do I have to do everything?'

She released the latch that held the ironing board's legs extended, folded it and replaced it to its storage place.

'Great', he smiled, snubbing her stress. 'That means I can do the washing up quickly.'

'O for crying out loud!' Her voice no longer tinkled but grated in his stomach.

She stepped into the lounge, grabbed her purse and sunglasses.

'I have to go.'

'You said, five minutes.'

'I need you to be with me on this one, you promised to help me carry the box.'

'I will, I will.'

He gently lowered her favourite mug into the sink, turned on the hot water and splashed washing up liquid over the dirty dishes and cutlery. At his back, Harmony paced.

'Have you put cream on your face?' he asked her.

'Of course.'

'Have you packed your glasses?'

'Yes.'

'Have you got your passport?'

'Naturally.'

'What about that hand cream?'

'Yes, that is in my purse, too.'

'What about that scarf?'

'It's all there', she quibbled.

'Are you sure?'

As she checked one last time and found all items in their correct place, Horace dried his hands at the dishcloth that hung off the stove top.

'See, and while you are still checking, I am done.'

For the first time, Harmony smiled.

'But you have not buttoned up your shirt!'

Even while she spoke, he fumbled the buttons closed.

'How much time?'

'Two minutes.'

'See, we are on time! I really don't know why you are fussing like this. We have never been late yet!'

Harmony harrumphed. She pushed him towards the door, pulled the keys off the lock on the inside and handed them to Horace who dutifully locked the door of their apartment from the outside.

They moved along the corridor to the elevator.

Horace was the first to notice that the lights above each of the four lifts were not showing the floor levels the cabins were on. Then Harmony pointed out the sign.

They glanced at each other and reluctantly marched to the staircase.

'Ten floors. I hope by the time we get home that the lifts will be working again!'

Neither of them liked climbing stairs.

At the mezzanine level, they stopped to collect Harmony's box, a handsome, sizeable make-up case, black with silver accents, that Horace had promised to carry for his wife. It was heavier than it looked, and he was glad to do this favour for Harmony.

'Thanks, darling', Harmony piped as they made their way to the main entrance of their building.

Just as they were about to leave, their landlady entered.

'Harmony, Horace, so good to see you', she beamed. 'Do you have a moment? I have something I wanted to discuss with you.'

Horace, who hung back behind Harmony, tried to push on.

'We have to leave, I am awfully sorry, we are in a rush just now. We catch up when we get back.'

'No, no, it will only take a minute. Let me tell you ...'

The elderly landlady slipped a bulging bag off her shoulder. By the look of her, she had just returned from the beach, a little pink around the edges where the sunscreen had not caught properly. Her withering skin was in need of some nourishing after sun, and her sweaty body required a cooling shower.

'Please, Dorothy', Harmony started but free of her luggage, Dorothy blocked their way out and meaningfully nodded her head.

'Seriously, only a minute.'

Resigned, Harmony checked her watch. 2 minutes late already!

'You see, it's about the cockroaches.'

'Cockroaches? We don't have cockroaches. Have you seen any cockroaches, honey?' Horace tried to guide the conversation along, knowing that Dorothy could stretch any short story into a full-length novel.

'That is exactly my point. There are no cockroaches in this building. But for it to remain that way, we have to spray again, and we have to keep spraying.'

'So, what do you want from us?' Harmony, too, feared Dorothy's ability to stretch the most irrelevant snippets of information into major chunks of knowledge.

Interrupted, Dorothy looked from Horace to Harmony, trying to regroup her thoughts.

'We need someone to come and do it.'

'Pest Control, yes, just get someone.'

'Well, it will cost.'

'How much?'

'I don't know yet.'

'Well, find out and let us know. We really have to run now!'

Resolutely, Harmony pushed past the blockade that was Dorothy and hoped that Horace would follow.

'5 minutes late.'

'Honey, it will be alright, there is plenty of buffer in your planning. We have never been late yet.'

As she stepped onto the sidewalk, she held out her hand and immediately, a taxi stopped.

Horace unloaded his box and they scrambled into the backseat.

'Marina Mall, please.'

Slowly, the taxi inched into the evening traffic and made its way towards their destination.

Traffic on the Corniche was at a standstill. Harassed, Harmony checked her watch and checked again, while Horace chatted to the driver.

'Accident', she heard him say and thought 'please, not now!' as she sent a silent prayer to the powers above, hoping that they would comply with her wish for a speedy trip to the mall.

The taxi inched its way forward, her heart beating away the minutes.

She was supposed to have arrived at Marina mall already, she reluctantly admitted to herself.

Sideways, Horace searched her face. He knew her too well; he knew how delicately she planned these engagements and how important time keeping was to her. Her client would not stand for her being late and would rescind the contract. Harmony had high hopes for this particular deal, and with the money she got paid, they would be in a good position to leave town, go for a long vacation before settling elsewhere in the world.

Harmony had been complaining about the heat. It was only early June, and yet temperatures were above 40 degrees Celsius already. The summer would be hot and long, and she suffered. A vacation at this point would be nice, so Horace joined Harmony in her silent prayers.

Two traffic lights before the bridge to Marina Mall, as their taxi slowed for the changing lights, a small silver Honda ran straight into the back of them.

Harmony burst into tears.

'Princess don't cry. This is not your fault', Horace tried to console her, but she refused to listen to his calming voice.

As the drivers got out of their cars, stopping all traffic yet again, they decided that they should not wait for the police.

They stepped outside; Horace motioned the driver to open the slightly concertina'd trunk of his Toyota while Harmony paid him double what showed on the clock.

'Police coming', the driver tried to protest, but Harmony and Horace, swinging the box over his shoulder as if it was weightless, strode towards the next set of traffic lights in the hope of finding a taxi to take them across the bridge.

'I have never been this late in my life', Harmony panted.

'It will be alright', Horace insisted not for the first time. There was nothing else to say.

Sweat was pouring down their backs when they reached the next taxi stop where a long line of people was already waiting.

Positioning herself just before the taxi bay, Harmony waited for the next taxi that was dropping off passengers and before anybody could object, climbed into the back seat with the box while Horace sat in the front. Either ignored the anger of those they left behind waiting. Instead, Horace showed the driver a 20 dirham note.

'Marina Mall, please hurry.'

The man smiled, indicated and put his foot on the gas pedal to the floor as the cars in the main flow applied breaks and honked indignantly.

They did not slow for changing lights and reached Marina Mall a few minutes later.

Horace grabbed the box, Harmony adjusted her blouse, and they as much as ran into the air-conditioned building.

They hurried past shops advertising the latest reductions in time for the Ramadan sales, past shoppers enjoying a leisurely afternoon. There was no more time to lose, the entire buffer of one hour that Harmony had included in her calculations to make the appointment on time had been used up.

They panted heavily by the time they reached the elevator to the tower. There was no wait, the doors opened as they walked up, spitting out visitors from the coffee shop and vistas high above.

They were alone as they ascended.

'You will be alright. Just breathe, honey', he whispered as he rested his hand on the low of her back.

Harmony simply nodded.

At the level of the coffee shop, they exited. Horace went to sit and wait for Harmony to finish her engagement, while Harmony slipped into the rest rooms. Nerves always made her need to empty her bladder.

She ran cold water over the back of her hands and splashed some drops into her face.

Then she stood straight, ran her fingers through her hair and smiled at her reflection in the mirror. This little exercise always helped her reign in her anxiety.

The box strap slung over her right shoulder; she made her way to the upper level. The former restaurant stood empty for renovations that had been parked due to the turn down in the economy. The space was empty and inviting, the views uninterrupted across Abu Dhabi and the Marina far below.

From her purse, she pulled her special spectacles. Not only did they provide protection against the glare of the sun, they also magnified her field of vision by a factor of ten. Unsteadily due to the momentary blur of her vision, she walked towards the windows. It took her a moment before she managed to orientate herself and found the villa and docking area she was looking for.

'You are late', Harmony had not heard the man approach. 'What kept you?'

Not turning away from the window, she shrugged.

'I am here now.'

He glanced at his watch, shimmering golden and expensive on his hairy wrist.

'You can do it?'

She nodded.

'You got everything?'

Another nod.

She stepped aside and opened a window into a different direction. From the box, she took the pieces of her rifle and attached the high definition scope.

The man gasped.

'What are you doing? This is the wrong boat!'

'I am doing my job.'

She aimed at a tree far away and used the miss to adjust the new scope.

'You got my money?' She asked before she moved back into her previous position.

'Yes' he gasped, marvelling at her calmness. With the eye of a connoisseur, he ogled her equipment.

'Can I see that?' There was something in his voice that she did not like.

'Are you trying to keep me now from doing what I am supposed to be doing?'

'Of course not. Just ignore me: Do not let me keep you.'

She settled the rifle, adjusted the mechanism and aimed. Before pulling the trigger, she stopped.

'What are you doing here anyways? Your presence was not part of the deal as far as I remember.'

'I was waiting for you downstairs, but you did not show on time and I wondered ...'

He did not finish his sentence as the rifle popped. With the silencer, there was hardly any noise.

The man stood with his mouth open as Harmony showed him that the scantily clad woman on his yacht had collapsed. She had hit her target.

He tried to speak but no words were formed that Harmony could understand.

'My money?' She held her hand out.

He placed an envelope into it, and she smoothly dropped it into her purse.

'Nice watch', she admired as she unclipped it from his wrist. As he tried to object, she tripped him and with a surprised exclamation, he fell through the open window to the roof far below. There was a loud thump, but the glass did not break. Unless somebody had seen him drop, it would be a while before he would be discovered.

Unhurriedly, Harmony replaced the pieces of her rifle into its cotton carrier, took off her gloves. She was sorry to leave the new scope behind: that had cost a lot of money, but it was better this way.

'Have you enjoyed your cappuccino?' She asked of Horace minutes later. As he took the now empty beauty case from her, he noted its light weight.

'How did it go?' He asked, left eyebrow raised.

She shrugged and smiled.

'He tried to keep me, but he paid the price. The ultimate price. In the end.'

Then, she handed Horace the Rolex.

'Another one for your collection, darling', she cooed as, arm in arm and without hurry, they leisurely started their journey back to their apartment.

Lucky

I killed a man."

He said this calmly, his voice clear, his body relaxed lying on the bed next to me, spent by my side.

We had met, if you want to call it that, no more than a couple of hours ago. Tired and with another six-hour drive ahead of me, I had not fancied driving into the night and had pulled into one of those service stations that had everything: pumps, a brightly-lit restaurant, and a dusty motel up a short hill.

He was stopped at the pump next to mine and our eyes met across our vehicles. His was a black affair, powerful against my small red thing. He nodded at me, raised a hand to an imaginary hat and my mind raced to evaluate the opportunities.

He went in to pay and by the time my car was full up, he was already back at his. My hopes faded till I returned from paying and noticed he was still there, ignoring the honking line building behind, urging him on. He did not look at me, his face turned straight ahead. I got in and drove to the parking lot of the restaurant a few yards ahead. He pulled in two or three cars away.

The restaurant was one of those efficient self-serve deals and as my stomach rumbled, I grabbed not only a coffee but also a cream cheese bagel. To hell with carbs late in the evening! I was about to indulge, and needed the calories.

He was taller than me, skinny but built, with muscles that came from work rather than working out. His face spoke to me, kind but haunted, a bad-boy turn-able-good kind-of look that I knew could drive me crazy with just a smile and a wink of his dark eyes. His jeans were faded, like his face well worn. His dark hair was cropped short and on closer inspection, now that we had the neon lights of the eating place to our disadvantage, there was a smattering of grey all over. I judged him to be in his late 40s, just like myself.

I chose a quiet corner, away from through-traffic and he positioned himself at the next table, facing me. We ate in silence, but I felt my face flush from the thoughts he had started in my mind, and he smiled and nodded again.

This time, I nodded back. The deal was done.

We completed our meals in silence, left about half the food behind as adrenaline accelerated us.

I got into the car, parked at the motel, checked in. He was steps behind. I asked for a room one flight up. I don't know what he asked for, but he got the room next to mine.

During the short ride in the lift, we did not look at each other, neither did we speak. As I unlocked the door to my room, he put the key in his, gave a wistful nod towards my door, a shy smile in my direction. Then he was gone.

I set my bags down, hurriedly brushed my teeth and before I could sit on my bed, wondering if I had understood him right, there was a knock.

I opened, he pushed in, the door fell closed. His lips on mine, his arms pulling me in hard, he did not have to push to get me to bed. Clothes came off, I cannot remember whether he tore off mine and I his, or if we both did our own.

The sex was unforgettable. I no longer was tired.

Afterwards, we lay there, evaluating the paint on the ceiling.

"I killed a man."

I let the echo of his words resound in my mind and gave it a blink's notice before I turned and kissed him on the lips. Carefully, with something that in other circumstances could have felt like love. He responded.

Our love making this time was less hurried, and he took great care of me. The lights were on, our eyes locked into each other. Our fingers entwined; our bodies moved in unified pleasure.

We did not speak. Words would have messed it all up.

We were hungry and took our fill.

He was the kindest man I had ever been with. When we were done, he held me, and I felt his breath on my hands as he brushed his lips against my fingers. He did not fall asleep, he stayed awake with me through the night. He was different, so very different from all the others.

At first light, he stood and walked into the bathroom. I heard the toilet flush, and the shower start.

Quickly, I put my clothes on, grabbed my things.

On the dresser lay his watch, his wallet and a grizzled leather bracelet. As I walked out the door, I snatched that bracelet and headed for my car. I hit the road but pulled off at the next exit: I did not want him to follow and find me.

In a small, dark layby, I scanned the bracelet. The fear that they would send someone after me was always there, but the temptation of a male body was simply too great. His face had spoken just the right words, that first moment of meeting had been so perfect, I had wondered if he had been sent specifically to catch me. But there was no tracker on the leather strap.

I wrapped the bracelet around my wrist and raised my arm to appreciate its simple beauty. I would wear this now. I would wear this till the next lucky one.

"I killed a man."

I had to smile. How would he have reacted if I had told him? What could I have said?

'Don't worry, you get used to it' or 'it gets easier after the second one' somehow would have killed the moment and could have opened up a weird kind of conversation.

As I drove off, I thought of the treasures hidden in their small compartment below the glove box. Watches, bracelets, rings. Man's things. My trophies. I smiled: I wondered what he would have said if he had known how

close he had been to be the next. I pushed down hard on
the accelerator. Lucky.

The First Death of Evi B.

In the bowling alley of life, the generations stand at the top of their lanes, waiting for the approaching thump-clunk of the ball that spells the end of their existence. With an ear-splitting crash, one after the other falls, leaving the remainder of friends, those that they grew up with and have known for most of their lives, wondering when it would be their turn.

There are times when only one pin is left, standing alone, counting breaths and listening to the thump-clunk on neighbouring lanes: remembering the faces of those already fallen. Anxious, hopeful. Great-grandmother was the last of her generation. She did not mind, but every morning, she was surprised that Death had not visited in the night to fetch her away. Then, at 93, her time came and one day she heard the bowling ball approaching that carried her name. Kerchunk, kerchunk, and she fell, glad that it was finally over. Her lane now is empty and slowly slides into oblivion '*exit stage left*', while on the far side new generations are added '*enter stage right*'.

Every so often, something goes awry and the ball flicks over to a lane it was not meant to touch, hitting a life-pin of a younger generation, a generation whose turn had not quite yet come. This is what happened to Auntie G who died from blood cancer in her thirties. 'Far too young', as the priest told the congregation at her funeral. In 2000, it hit Uncle H like a stray bullet on a straight road. Those of the older generations of the adjoining lanes wrinkled their faces, shook on their solid bases and almost tumbled over from the shock of it.

And then there are the times when a pin is struck, falls over, spins indeterminably and miraculously straightens itself. And that is what happened to Evi B.

* * *

A normal weekday morning, the children at school, her husband at work, and yet Evi felt somewhat strange. This was her fourth pregnancy, and without being able to be specific, it had not been like the others.

This one should have been better: the conditions were safe now that they were in their own home, the war was over and they had enough food to eat since the men worked and there was money coming in constantly. But no. She could not rest, the baby kicking at her, turning restlessly inside her womb. Morning sickness that lasted most of her days, cramps and general un-wellness. Two more months, she hoped, and then they would be blessed with a fourth and final little B. Evi could not wait but knew she had to.

She wiped down the kitchen counter. No longer being able to bend, she waited for her mother to come and wash the floors. O, she was blessed having family so close by! Her husband's mother only upstairs, a call away if she felt a need; her own parents no more than a block away and checking in daily.

Evi hummed a song she had heard on the radio the other day. She missed dancing, but two months more and then she would be able to do it again, waltz and polka around their spacious kitchen. She had insisted on a big kitchen just for this reason: the kitchen was the heart of a house, always has been and always will be.

She turned and took it all in: the new furniture, the table and chairs.

Yes, it had been worth it.

With a frown, she noted that there were still crumbs on the table from the breakfast and as she chided herself for being so neglectful, she walked across. Halfway, the baby kicked viciously and Evi paused.

A wetness slithered down her leg and when she leant forward to see over her bump, horror struck her at the blood that was pooling by her feet. She tried to turn to make for the door to call for help, but in the dampness, she slipped and fell, bumping her head.

With her last thoughts she hoped that her mother would clean the table before the children and her husband returned for lunch. *O God, what will they eat? I have not started cooking yet!*

* * *

During his routine morning walk, Evi's father decided to pop in to check on his oldest child and found her, lifeless, in a pool of blood in the middle of her kitchen. A man of few words, he raised the alarm. An ambulance was called and by the time they took her away, her parents were on their way to the hospital, leaving her husband's parents at the house.

'Don't let the children see this', he said to her mother-in-law, pointing at the reddish-brown mess that was congealing on the shiny tiles. She nodded.

'Don't worry, I take care of it.'

Evi's husband was called at work. His boss nodded and Ferd ran.

His breath ran ragged as he collapsed into his father-in-law's arms in the waiting rooms.

'Where is she? What happened?'

Handing him a glass of tepid water, the old man tried to get Ferd to sit, but Ferd was far too anxious. His palms were sweating, not just from running, but because he was scared. *'Evi, Evi, where are you?'* his spirit called, but there was only darkness and even before the doctor came, he started to cry.

'Mr B?'

The man looked efficient in his white coat. It flapped open, revealing a light blue shirt and darker tie underneath. There was a splash of red on the shirt and Ferd could not avert his eyes. His Evi's blood? He wanted to stretch out his arm, let his fingers touch it, but his brain did not send the right command and his hand dangled ineffectively by his side.

'Mr B, the news is not good. You have to make a choice: we can save the baby, or we can save your wife. We cannot save both.'

With eyes wide in torment, Ferd stared unseeingly at the doctor.

'Excuse me, I am Evi's father', the old man intervened. 'Surely! This is the 1950s, there must be a way?'

Saddened, the doctor shook his head in a negative.

'Mr B, you need to make a decision. Now. Otherwise, I cannot guarantee ...', leaving the words hanging in the sterile space of the hospital waiting room.

Ferd swallowed.

'I have three children at home. Please, save my wife.' *'She is the love of my life'*, he added in his head. *'Without her, I cannot live'*, but these words none of those standing around him heard.

The doctor nodded, turned, and hurried back to the operating theatre.

* * *

An hour passed. The Mother sitting in a quiet corner, silently praying. The Father pacing up and down, frowning. The Husband sitting, his elbows on his knees, his hands folded, silently crying.

The doors swung open once more and the doctor approached. His face grey and taut, his eyes red rimmed as if he had been crying.

'I am so sorry', he almost whispered, his voice failing.

The Husband looked up, nodded.

'A nurse will come and be with you shortly. I need a moment to write out the certificate.'

They all cried. The Father put a hand on the Husband's shoulder.

'Will you wait here, with me?'

'Of course. And we will come home with you. Afterwards.'

But instead of waiting in the cold white waiting room that now looked foreboding and dim, Ferd made his way to the chapel where he fell on his knees to pray.

'Lord Father, I don't know why you punish me and take away my Evi. How can I tell the children that their mother is gone? How can I carry on without my Evi? I am not strong. Lord Father help me! Show your mercy! And if there is anything you can do, don't let this be true. Give me my Evi back, I do whatever you ask of me!'

He cried, his spirit screaming and convulsing in sadness and fear of a life without his wife.

Ferd did not see or hear the two shadowy figures a few pews behind him.

The taller one sighed.

'You got it wrong, you know that don't you?'

The shorter one smiled.

'Well, what you gonna do about it?'

'We told you, today you are here for one. You hear? For one soul, not two!'

A snigger from the vibrating darkness by his side.

'Sorreeeee. My fault!' The cynicism in his voice was ripe with disdain for the spirit by his side.

'Yes, and this is why you need to give back that second soul.'

With a nod to the crying man in front, the Angel continued.

'That of the wife. You heard the man. He needs her; the children need her. She has a job to do still, her time has not come.'

Death cringed and sniffled.

'O come on! I was having fun!'

'See that man? How he is crying? That is NOT fun!'

'I don't like you. You have no sense of ... o, I don't know. Playing with you is hopeless!'

'You know that there is no way that God will allow this to happen, do you?'

Death shrugged: it was out of his hands already; he had done his job efficiently.

'I took two souls, and I already passed them on. Giving one back is going to mean paperwork ... who is going to do that?'

The Angel turned and stared at where Death's eyes should have been.

'You are kidding, right?'

There was something different about Death and the Angel stared in disbelief.

'Are you wearing make-up?'

And then, sniffing: 'And perfume?'

Death giggled childishly.

'Told you, I am having fun.'

With one last glance at Ferd in the front pew, the Angel made one last suggestion.

'Tell you what: I go and get Evi back, and you make sure her soul is ready.'

To Death, that sounded not like fun but ultimately fair, given that he could not go where Evi already was preparing for the next part of her journey. He held out his hand, for the Angel to shake, but the Angel snorted in disgust.

'I don't think so.' They left.

* * *

The meadow was of the juiciest, brightest, most beautiful green that Evi had ever seen. She stood in the middle of it, wondering how she had gotten there. But then she was overwhelmed by the ethereal beauty of her surroundings. She raised her arms wide and turned. There was nothing but this luscious green-ness.

'*The cows would love this*', she thought, then remembered that the cows were no longer hers to care for.

She turned and turned around her own axis, drinking the utter happiness that moved through her, getting drunk on her euphoria and the motion. Faster and faster.

Blue sky above her, cloudless, endless.

Green under her feet, soft, gentle.

She was in heaven! This was her heaven!

She slowed and, in the distance,, she perceived a light so bright that it was like the sun. Only, it was not the sun, it was better: this light did not hurt her eyes. She did not have to shield her face as she watched the light coming closer.

'Evi', it greeted her.

'Father?'

'Welcome.'

She turned again, with a sweep of her arms embracing the meadow.

'Is this heaven?'

'Yes, my child, this is heaven. Your heaven.'

'I like it. But where are the others?'

'Well', the voice started, but there was something reverberating within it that made her pause.

'Well', the voice started again, 'there was some mistake. Even here, sometimes there are mistakes. You should not be here: our records show that it is not your time yet. But then, on the other hand, you are already here.'

Confused, Evi looked around.

Mistakes? In Heaven? Who would have thought?

'You like it here?'

She nodded.

'Well', the voice came slowly and haltingly so that Evi had time to think while it spoke. 'You have a choice. You can stay here and wait for the right time. Or, you can go back and all will be as before.'

Evi turned around slowly.

This was the most beautiful meadow she had ever seen. The green was so dense, it stilled her hunger. It refreshed her. It cleared her mind.

'And my baby?'

'No, not the baby.'

Evi nodded.

'I understand.'

'The decision is yours. Whatever you chose will be alright with us.'

'Will I remember this meadow? Will I remember talking to you?'

God paused for effect.

'As long as you promise not to tell the world, or they will all want to come and see.'

He smiled. He knew her answer before he had asked her: he knew that Evi had to go back, for her husband, her children, and those that she had not yet met. He knew she loved the looks of the meadow, but that deep in her heart, this would not fulfil her eternity: not yet.

* * *

The nurse came running.

'Doctor?'

He turned. Tired, worn out, it was time that his duty finished, and he could go home to his own wife and children. There had been too much drama today already.

'Yes, Nurse?'

'Doctor, please, come. Right now!'

She was breathless. Her face was flushed.

'What is it?'

'Please, it is urgent!'

'Well, hold on, if it is not a question of life and death, I want to hand this death certificate to Mr B first, so they can start ...'

'NO!'

The nurse's scream made him stop.

'Don't give him that certificate, for heaven's sake: his wife is NOT dead!'

'What?'

He stood, open mouthed, gawping at her.

'She is not dead?'

At her insistence, he allowed her to guide him to the room where they kept the dead, before fixing them for the family to see one last time. He glanced at his watch. 45 minutes ago, he himself had asked the nurses to take Mrs B to that room: her body too much of a mess for her husband and parents to see her, blood everywhere like after a day of slaughter at the farm.

'She must be dead!'

The nurse shaking her head, pulling him along.

'I know. We all checked her pulse, we all wanted her to live. There was no pulse, no breath, nothing. We left her and just now, as we pushed in old Mrs M who had passed in her sleep, there was movement and a moan from Mrs B. Can you imagine? That new trainee nurse, she got such a fright! And when I checked, Mrs B opened her eyes, smiled and asked when she could go home!'

Still speechless, the nurse led the doctor into a cold and clammy room, where a gaggle of nurses and attendants were huddled around Evi who struggled to sit up.

They all hushed as the doctor stepped near. His tears now tears of joy and gladness; gladness at being wrong;

gladness at being able to tell her husband that she was alive, that there had been a mistake.

'Mrs B', he greeted her as he grabbed for her wrist, bruised and purple from the catheters and earlier injections.

Her pulse was strong and regular.

'May I please check you out really quick?'

With a nod of his head he sent all but the head nurse away.

'We thought you were dead', he gently approaches a difficult subject.

'I know', Evi admitted.

'You know?'

Evi fell back onto her hospital crib.

'I know.'

She closed her eyes, feeling her heart beat strong and steady, alive with her pulse and full of a new spirit.

* * *

'Mr B?'

The doctor approached, a sheen on his face that Evi's family could not place. Surely, the doctor would not come and talk to them about her death with a smile on his face?

'I have something to tell you …'

* * *

'The big man himself! I am honoured!' Death pretended to spit on the hospital floor, but as he had no bodily fluids, it was nothing but a hollow gesture.

'Good managers check on their workforce, didn't you know?'

Death frowned. He shook, his anger seething. He hated being reminded that he was nothing better than a lackey to the big man.

'It is all right now. Evi is back.'

'I hate you', he squeezed out with gritted teeth, throwing darts of spite at the retreating back of light.

'I know', God whispered, just loud enough for Death to hear.

* * *

And so, Evi got to heal in the hospital for a week, her husband seeing her with renewed love, the children sad that their new sister now would not be playing with them after all.

Death stands by, waiting.

He watches her pin grow old and dusty, sees the many times when he could have thrown that bowling ball, or even a tennis ball – anything to topple her. But whenever he wants to sneak a closer look at her, there is the spirit of an Angel or even the Big Man himself, watching out for Evi.

Slowly, he picks off one after the other around her, toying. He knows that she has seen him, and that she no longer fears what he can do to her. He hates her for that. He hates her for knowing of her heaven, knowing of the greenest meadow there ever was.

Death stands and polishes that bowling ball, just for Evi.

And he knows that his time will come.

Ways to Disappear

A disastrous weekend.

And yes, it had been my idea.

I wish I had not suggested this quick get-away into the Scottish heartland, but here it is.

Ken had not liked inviting my German friend anyway, and I feared that if we stayed in our tiny apartment, he would burst. He could get quite angry at times, and I did not want to spoil my friendship with the German girl. So I had decided to initiate this get away.

The nice hotel down by the Loch we could not afford. Not after he had just spent the last three weeks with his children who leeched off him big way. Yet again. We found a small B&B, where we shared the moldy bathroom with some English family, and the beds were so clammy at night that it took ages to get warm. Typical Scotland, in a way. Don't get me wrong, I love Scotland, but there is something about their B&Bs. That, though, is another story altogether.

That morning, the sun was out. The fields of heather shone in typically postcard-from-Scotland style as we chose our tour for the day. Being German, my friend had checked out the area in her guidebook and she suggested that with weather like this, we should drive to the Loch and climb the mountain which offered a most fantastic panorama from its top.

Ken in his usual Ken-ish way lorded it over her and in his best teacher voice told her that it was not a mountain and that 'mountains' in Scotland were called Ben or ... and here I interrupted because it really did not matter. He could be such a pain in the posterior, really!

But my friend took the admonition in her stride and Ken smiled at her sweetly, so after another pot of dark, strong tea, we set out.

Ken parked the old Volvo by the Loch and we prepared for the long walk uphill. Now, I am an okay walker, but uphill is always a struggle, particularly when I am on the mood medication and just getting over yet another exploratory operation. There were no stitches left, but I still was sore, and I asked repeatedly to slow down.

He really did not cope well with me being unfit like this, and just to annoy me even more, he hooked his arm under my friend's and so openly flirted with her that it hurt inside. I cringed. My friend threw me questioning glances, but I simply smiled. I could not let him win this round! I was so much better than this pettyish fight we had when he returned from his vacation with the children and I found his bank book.

The walk uphill was not too bad. The well-posted path led through woodland. There was enough space between the trees to allow for good views of the Loch and the posh hotel below. It was a steady incline, and once I set my mind to it, I was able to keep pace. The two of them slightly in front of me set the speed. Their laughter rang crystal clear and grated my insides. I was so pleased they had a good time and got on so well, I secretly devised plans to spoil their twosomeness. The more I thought about it, the less of a clue I had.

We walked for a couple of hours, stopping to sip water every so often and taking photos of the trees who never were apart enough to allow the camera to take proper photos of the beautiful expanse of water below. Thank goodness for digital photography, I remember thinking, at least I don't have to pay to print the results. At that stage, I no longer cared what my 'friend' would make of it.

Suddenly, the terrain changed, and the trees made way to a stoney flatness that marked the 2/3 way up to the top. I was exhausted and the non-stitches hurt. My insides convulsed and I felt faint.

My friend commented on the whiteness of my face, but I simply smiled. Ken ignored me, and then his eyes threw me a challenge to speak up. I kept silent. To hell with him!

We rested, but when she took out the guidebook, we were informed that the remainder of the way to the top would be really quite steep.

'You know what, I don't think I can manage', I began my excuse.

'I want to reach the top', Ken stated.

'I bet you do, bastard', I mumbled just loud enough for myself to hear.

He smirked at me.

Then he turned to my friend.

'Are you up for it?' He asked of her and she blushed, purposely misunderstanding his meaning. Or was she? Did he know how his words could be misinterpreted? Idiot. I had enough of his innuendos.

'Here', I handed the friend my camera. 'You go ahead, you take photos from the top, and I meet you at the car.'

'Are you sure?'

'Of course, go ahead.'

I smiled sweetly and waved them off.

The idea only came when I started walking downhill. There were a few others coming up from the same carpark where we had left the car, but then the forest around me fell silent. The only thing interrupting the eerie quiet were my own footsteps.

Would it not be easy to just disappear? Nobody would see, nobody would know where I had gone. They might use tracker dogs, but then ... one good rainfall, and not much of my tracks would be left. All I had to do was veer off the path and I would come out miles away from the car park. Or I could reach the old rusty Volvo and keep on walking towards the Loch. At the end of summer, the water would be cold, but I was sure that I could cope with that. I mean, I had swum other lakes up to early October, so this should be do-able. I would reach the water and keep on going. The Loch was not that wide, and even with some currant, I could probably reach the other side. Well, maybe not – it would take me too long, I no longer was a strong swimmer and I was wearing clothes and shoes that I would need on the other side. Damn, I should have prepared this! I should have dropped a change of clothes on the other side of the Loch. I should have brought my credit cards ... no, I should have emptied my account and deposited cash, hoping nobody would have found it before I reached.

The peace and stillness of the place had my heart racing and my mind boiling over with crazy idea. If only .... If only I had prepared!

I turned back to look behind me. Nobody in sight. Had they reached the top yet? Were they talking about me? What were they saying? Was he still flirting with her, now that I was no longer there to see and feel hurt?

Could I trust them? That was always the big question. That, and not really knowing what went on in people's heads. I mean, would they think that I thought about disappearing?

I stumbled and almost fell. Walking downhill was even worse for my non-stitches than uphill. I had to be careful. What if I fell? I would tumble and roll and not stop till I was at the road that went all the way around the Loch. Knowing my luck, just then a big lorry would come, and I would slip under its backwheels. That would have me disappear! The driver would not notice and I would *** whoosh *** just be gone.

Disappearing, yes, but not dying. I was not suicidal! I just wanted that rat of a husband to suffer a little bit, and that nasty friend to learn that she should not flirt with him, that it meant something that Ken and I were married, even though she kept breaking up with her boyfriends and ...

I had reached the car.

With my set of keys, I unlocked and climbed into the driver seat. I could simply drive away, leaving them stranded. I could disappear the car somewhere – there was a boat launch I had noticed earlier. If I set the car going, would it simply roll on and on? O heck.

I must have fallen asleep because I woke with a start when they knocked on the window.

I scrambled out, stretching and Ken wrapped me in his arms.

'Better, darling?'

I nodded.

'You must be exhausted. I guess this outing was too much for you. Let's get you back to the B&B.'

He hugged me close. I smelled his aftershave. Disappear? Yeah. Not likely!

The Specialist

I have dedicated my professional life to the safeguarding of people and their lives. There are worldwide very many of us who do similar jobs, but I have developed something of an additional specialism.

I give you an example: imagine a ladder resting against a wall. Now imagine you go up one step. If you fall off that first rung, what happens? Probably nothing very much other than you get a scare. Now imagine you go up further: two or three steps. If you fall now? You might hurt your wrists and elbows as you try and buffer your fall. If you slide off awkwardly, there might be damage to your legs, there certainly will be parts of your body that turn black and blue. But tell me: how far do you have to walk up a ladder before a fall could turn fatal? How far before it most definitely will end in your death?

There are countries in the world, where the protection of people on ladders is discussed in official rules and regulations. But somebody had to work up the basis for these laws. People like me.

This is only an example to give you an idea. But, you see, in more ways than most imagine, I am a specialist in death.

Many years ago, I fell into a niche. It was a development that I had not planned, having been rather busy forging my standard professional career.

It was in the early 2000s, and I shared an office with a quiet design engineer. Darryl. He hardly ever spoke about anything other than work, but one morning, Darryl was beside himself.

His head bobbed like that of one of those wobbly-head dogs that were popular when I was a child in Germany, left to right, between his computer screen and the window out into the atrium. He muttered to himself, his hands in his lap.

'Darryl?' I quietly addressed him as I approached.

Darryl continued in his erratic movements, not listening, not hearing me.

'Darryl?' I called louder.

I closed the door to our office with a bang that made him shudder and his head spun towards me.

His eyes brim-full of tears that did not want to fall, he looked at me, unseeing.

'Darryl? What is wrong?'

I huddled down in front of him, so that I had to look up to his face. I did not want to intimidate him.

Darryl sighed.

'Tell me?'

He shook his head left to right, faster and faster, till he managed to squeeze out an unnecessary 'No!' His motion was making me dizzy.

'I don't think you are okay. Do you want me to call somebody?'

At that, his tears started flowing freely. Like a kid, he swiped at them with the back of his hand. Snot bubbled from his nose; he wiped it away with his shirt sleeve.

His eyes forlornly focused on me, he started mumbling. It took some time before I realised he was repeating the same words over and over again.

'She's gone', I thought I could hear him say.

'Who's gone?'

Eventually, he stopped mid-motion. There was a deep inhale, as if his lungs were empty and needed filling up with the desperation of the starving, then it erupted: how his girlfriend of four years had packed her things, then told him that she had found somebody else, who was taller, funnier and better than him. With no prior signs that he had ever seen, she had left the previous evening, leaving Darryl in a heap.

I was about to tell him that things weren't definite, that he would find his feed again before long, and that a brand-new dating scene awaited him, when Darryl turned away from me. His next words chilled me to the core.

'I am going to kill myself!'

My mind raced. What to say? What to do?

'How?'

My unexpected question brought his attention back to our conversation.

'What?'

'I said, how are you planning to do it?'

His tears had stopped.

'Why?'

'I want to make sure that I am not the one finding you.'

He stopped to consider this.

Then he looked outside where a milky sun lit the atrium a fraction brighter than the electrical lightbulbs did.

'I am going to jump out the window.'

By that point, my mind had already switched into gear. I was a problem solver: no problem was too tricky to be solved by a few good questions and answers.

'This window?'

Darryl shrugged.

I shook my head.

'We are on the third floor.'

'So?'

'Not high enough. You might end up breaking all your bones. If you really want to kill yourself, you need to be higher up.'

Another glance out of our windows.

'How high?'

'I would go as high as 7th floor, or even higher.'

He seemed to mull this over.

'Accounts are on the 8th floor. I could go there.'

Darryl considered his wristwatch.

'They all go for lunch around 11:30. I could do it then.'

He seemed almost keen.

'Do their windows open?'

'They have windows like we do.'

'You should pick a window that faces out, not the atrium.'

'Why not the atrium?'

'Think about it. If you fall through, the glass will cut you to shreds. That hurts you and damages everybody who sees the result. If you don't fall through, it won't be high enough.'

'Damn, you are right.'

'But do the windows open wide enough?'

'I told you, they have windows like we do!'

'When is the last time you opened our windows?'

At this, Darryl stood and pushed open the window closest to him. There was a gap wide enough to put his hand through, wide enough to increase the flow of air, but certainly not wide enough to jump through.

'Shit!' Darryl said.

'You better go and check.'

'I could just call?'

'You should go yourself. Take a notepad and write down all the possibles.'

Darryl rummaged in his desk drawer for a pen, grabbed his notebook and made to leave but turned.

'Thanks.'

'Don't worry.'

And I did not worry either. Darryl took the next few hours checking all the windows, with eventually two results: both of us were surprised that nobody asked him what he was doing, checking all the windows from the 8th floor up. Secondly, by the end of it, he no longer felt the need to jump.

A few weeks after this episode, Darryl got a transfer. I never saw him again but from a mutual acquaintance I know that he got married. Maybe a year later, I had an email from somebody I did not know. As introduction, the email started with 'Darryl said to contact you'. Over time, more and more emails arrived, and I created a special email address. Now, I have a second phone just for these calls.

They all start with 'Darryl said to contact you', it is the secret code important to understand the importance of the call.

I never advertised my services, never charged, never handed out that email address or the phone number. But over the years, I have become a Consultant in Death.

As I do not know most of my clients in person, I cannot tell you how successful I am. But since they pass on my contact details, I am sure that they decide after talking to me to pursue other means of coping. Because, if they did not listen to what I was really telling them, they would be dead and could no longer hand out my information.

Once or twice I received thank you notes, but nothing else.

My day job keeps me busy, and there are times when I do not check my Inbox and leave my second phone turned off. There are times when I don't even think about my special services. I need to protect myself. My sanity.

Two weeks ago, I was home with a broken ankle. I spent most of my time on the couch, watching daytime TV and reading. From sheer boredom, I switched on that second telephone.

To my great surprise, it rang within half an hour.

I swiped the green arrow and held the phone to my ears without saying anything.

A woman's voice said: 'The guy who gave me this number said to mention that Darryl said to contact you. I hope that means something to you.'

I froze in shock. I bolted straight upright.

I could not get any words out.

'Hello?'

I pictured her. Late 30s, blond. A professional. Married, no children. I remembered her happy smile from the Christmas cards she sent every year showing her and her husband, the dogs, the pony.

My sister.

'Are you there?'

I coughed in reply.

'I want to kill myself. I have tried before, twice, and if I fail again this time, my husband will put me into a clinic where they will give me drugs so I can no longer think. I would lose myself to a fate worse than death. Please, my friend told me that you could help me get it right.'

'Sally?'

She stopped, inhaled.

'Patsy?'

'Sally, why do I not know that you have tried to commit suicide before?'

She disconnected. I dialled her number. Sally did not pick up.

I tried again and again.

I considered calling her husband, but what would I have said? I could divulge neither her plea nor my involvement.

Eventually, Sally called me on my official line.

'Pat ... I don't know what to say.'

'Sis, why don't I know? Why would you call a stranger and not talk to me?'

We cried together.

'I did not know I was calling you!'

'That is not the point!'

'Pat, I want to die. Help me or I jump in front of a train!'

I bit my tongue. Suddenly, I wanted to know more. I wanted to know how my beautiful little sister could feel this bad that she should consider ending her life. There were times in the past when we both had felt depressed, but we always had each other, even when our parents died, and the world seemed to end. Why?

All Sally would tell me was that she would go to the station and jump in front of a train.

'Is it your husband? Is he making you unhappy?'

'No, of course not. We are as happy as we were on the first day!'

'Then why? Do you need money? I can send you money, if that is your problem!'

But all the issues I could think of, none were of any bother to her.

All she would come back to was ending her own life.

'Why, Sally?'

But she no longer heard me, she already told me that she would leave for the station immediately.

'Let me call you back on the other line, don't go yet.'

'Why?'

I lied a little.

'I need a bathroom break. And you know that with my ankle, walking takes a while. I call you back from the other phone in ten minutes. Will you wait that long?'

In my head I had a picture of her, thinking. Sally could be stubborn, but then agreed.

'Ten minutes?'

'Ten minutes.'

What to do? How could I convince her not to jump in front of a train or do anything else? I knew my little sister well enough; she would pull this through as a matter of principal.

When she picked up on the first ring, I got straight to the point.

'You realise that you have to time it right, right?'

'What are you talking about?'

'You said you wanted to jump in front of a train, did you not?'

Sally agreed.

'Then I am saying, you have to be careful not to mess it up. You have to time it right and jump in a certain way.'

'I just jump, and then ...'

'You see, this is what I mean. You can't just jump. It's not that simple. There are two ways. For both you are better off with a train that does not stop and is in full motion. You either jump onto the tracks and make sure that your head and most of your body is on the tracks, not in the part between. If you lie flat between the tracks, on the wooden things, you know what I mean? Then the train will go across you and you survive. Therefore, make sure your head lies on the metal, and if you can leave most of the rest of you on that part of the tracks as well, then you will end up mash but well dead. The second way you can do it, but that requires really good timing, is when the train is almost there and you jump against its front. That pulverizes you. You will travel a mile in small bits, nothing more than particles of blood, but there is no way you could survive this.'

'Fuck', Sally exclaimed. 'Does that hurt?'

'I am sure you die pretty quickly. But you need good nerves to do it properly, because you have to wait for the right time to jump. If you hit the side of the moving train, you might slip off and fall into the gap between platform and moving vehicle, and that is survivable.'

She considered.

'I don't know. I cannot do it. I am not brave enough.'

Before I could take a breath and move on, Sally came with another question.

'How else could I do it? I don't want to live any more. I will end it. I will. You know me. I cannot live like this any longer.'

'Sally, tell me, what is so bad in your life that you no longer can cope?'

But again, she did not answer me.

'I could hang myself.'

I nodded, but before I could answer, Sally carried on.

'How long does that take? Can someone find me and stop me pulling it through? I don't want to go into the clinic, I don't want them to drug me, so I don't know anything anymore! I want my clear mind!'

There was panic in her voice, but also the tinkling of her voice, clear and lucid as always.

'If you tie the knot properly, you will break your neck. That takes a good jump if you place the noose correctly. You need good rope, and a good place. If you go into the park, there are plenty of trees. Make sure you find a strong one: you don't want to jump off and then the branch to break off ...'

'I don't know how to tie a knot, so it breaks my neck.'

'Then it will take longer.'

'If I go into the woods, where nobody goes, I have time.'

'Yes. But there is another thing ...'

'Tell me!'

'Well, your bladder and your other muscles stop holding. You end up pissing and shitting yourself, and if you take your time dying, you will feel both run down your legs.'

'You are disgusting!'

'I am telling you the truth.'

'They said you were good.'

'I do what I can.'

I did not want to know whom she had spoken to. How she had gotten my phone number. None of my prior clients had ever been friends or family, not that I had realised.

After a moment, Sally surprised me with another question.

'How would you do it?'

'It?'

'Yes. If you were to end your life, kill yourself, how would you do it?'

Only once had I considered this question, so I had my answer ready.

'I would take my car and drive it at speed off a bridge.'

'There are fences and things, that is not possible!'

'When I thought this one out, I knew a place where they were working on a bridge. That would have been ideal.'

'And?'

'Obviously, I did not go ahead.'

'Why?'

I needed to keep her talking, I needed her to keep communicating. I was happy for her questions.

'I thought of those I would leave behind. I could not load that on my conscience.'

'There are no bridges where they are working on anywhere near me.'

'Then this option is out.'

'I don't have my car. When I tried the second time, they took my keys away.'

'Then that puts an end to taking your car and driving into a wall.'

'I want to kill myself.'

'I hear you. I cannot understand why you want to do this, but I hear you and I can hear your pain. Sally, why can't you tell me what is bothering you?'

'I need to end it all.'

'Can we pray together?'

As if in disgust, my little sister cried out.

'No. Faith means nothing to me!'

'I am sorry. I get a lot of strength from my prayers.'

'I don't. Not anymore. Tell me, or I just walk away.'

'You can jump off any bridge. The water is cold enough and you have only seconds before your heart will fail.'

'There are many bridges around here. Which one?'

'That is a decision that you will have to take.'

'Will you let me do it?'

'I cannot stop you. What do you think I should do?'

'You won't call my husband? You won't call the police?'

What options did I have? What did I want? What would I gain if my little sister ended up in a mental asylum, filled with drugs to the brim? I would have lost my sister any way.

'I won't call.'

'What will you do now?'

'I think I will put on my headphones and listen to some good music. I might hobble outside for a bit of a walk. Or maybe I make myself a big mug of hot cocoa and sit on the balcony in the cold.'

'But you will let me do what I want to do?'

'I hope that you will call me later and we talk some more.'

'Pats?'

'Yes, Sally?'

'Thank you.'

'Sally?'

'Yes, Pats?'

'I love you.'

But she had already disconnected.

The Food Thief

There are times when you can see things better. There are times when your vision clears up and all your senses are wide awake, and you notice. It's like your eyes and ears and taste buds have had a special clean. It's almost as if you suddenly have more senses than before. I guess I want to say that your instincts are awake. It does not happen all the time, and it is always followed by a dimming of the same senses and you go through life as if you are blind – seeing but not seeing, hearing but not hearing.

It was during one of those wide-awake-senses-time.

At first, it was an inkling that something was not as it should be.

I think it was the cookies.

Instead of five of those delicious, amazing treats, there were only four and crumbs left in the packaging.

You must think I am crazy, but I actually do count the cookies. I don't count the rice corns; I don't even weigh the rice. But cookies, slices of bread, pieces of chocolate – those items I count. Those items I count because they are luxuries, and luxuries are for special occasions only. That is how I noted that one cookie had turned into crumbs.

I was alone in the apartment, nobody else was going near my food supplies, and I knew I had not touched the cookies. How then could one of those precious treats have crumbled into ... when I brushed the remainders of that cookie into my hand, checking what was left, I noted that there was a lot less than a full cookie: about half of it was missing.

The remnants of the cookie, flavourful and aromatic, its richness not to be discarded lightly: when would I be able to buy cookies such as these ever again?

I tilted my head back and allowed the flakes of cookie to tumble onto my tongue. An explosion of sweetness, of delicious, comforting baking. I savoured the experience. I did not drink water for a long time, just so that flavour could stay and fill my mouth.

Four cookies left in the box. I re-taped the aluminium foil and replaced the sachet in the cupboard.

A few days later, I noted something wrong with the cornflakes. Before, I hated cornflakes. But now that there are no more shops selling them, I guard them eagerly and I eat no more than 15 of the golden-brown flakes at a time. And still, there seemed to be less than the last time I indulged.

I shrugged it off, thinking I was going crazy: being on your own too much does that to you, does it not?

And then, when I walked shoeless to the bathroom one morning, I trod on something that crackled underfoot. Surprised, I checked. Even more surprised I realised that I had trodden on a small piece of cornflake.

I knew that I had not wasted my cornflakes like that, knew that I had not spilled even the tiniest of pieces of one single baked flake onto the floor.

In the rising of a new day, I decided to search my apartment. My senses told me: I was not alone.

There are not that many spaces, so my food thief must have been small – but not too small since it managed to steal a cornflake from its box. Had the same thief also taken the cookie? What was I looking for? A rat? I wondered.

I searched high and low, disgusted and eager at the same time. It had been a long while since I had seen a rat. I wondered how big it would be, and what I should do when I found it.

During the day, I emptied and moved all the furniture, looked in all corners. I found nothing.

As night fell, I decided to stay awake.

I laid a trap – I took a cornflake, wetted it with some of the water from the bathing bucket, and laid it on the table.

I positioned my most uncomfortable chair so that I could see the object in the dark – the moon was out and illuminated my room if I did not draw the curtains. I sat and, in my head, listened to the songs of a bygone area, songs I used to dance to as a younger woman, songs I sang to when my friends organised karaoke. I waited.

I did not have to wait too long. Instead of a rat, it was a mouse. It was cute, lit up by the moon: a small, hairy body, a cute little snout, big, big ears, and a short tail. There it was, holding the flake between its front paws, nibbling away.

What to do?

I started talking; well, I whispered initially. I whispered non-sensical words, as if I was talking to a child, using a tone of voice that was soothing, calming, and wondered whether I could get to the mouse. I wanted to touch it, feel its hairy body, feel the heart of another living thing. Gingerly, I held out my hand and the mouse stopped to look at me.

It watched my hand, and then turned and our eyes met.

I hoped that my eyes told this little thing that I meant it no harm, that I was its friend, and that I had provided it this night's dinner. That, in fact, it should be thankful.

I held my hand close, and nervously, with twitching whiskers, it approached. I sat and waited, my hand resting on the table.

The mouse sniffed, turned away, came back, sniffed some more. I wriggled my fingers and it scampered, but I waited some more, and it came back. I guess it was hungry and wanted that cornflake. I laid the flake in my palm and after the longest time, during which my legs began to fall asleep on the uncomfortable chair, my nightly visitor returned and climbed into my palm.

The mouse felt warm, its hairs soft against my fingers.

As it grabbed the cornflake in its front paws, I gently closed my fingers to a cage and lifted the mouse, now captured in my hand, to my face. Calmly, I spoke to it: I welcomed it to my apartment, greeted it like a friend.

Through its hairy coat, I could feel its little heartbeat vigorously. I was surprised it did not bite me – if it had fought back with its probably very sharp teeth, I would have dropped it, but it sat unmoving in my hand, waiting like I had waited before.

For a while I played with the idea of keeping it as my pet. A cornflake a day – we could have been friends, could we not? Could you train mice? I am sure I could make it perform tricks. Wasn't there a movie about a mouse that never died that did just that: do tricks?

But then, I remembered what my teachers had told me about mice and rodents and with a flick of my thumb against its throat, I broke its neck.

Bloody food thief!

It had been a long time since I last had fresh meat. One bite, one single mouth full. I would chew well and enjoy the delicious luxury.

I stood, stretched, turned on the light, and went to the kitchen for a knife.

The Long Wait of Evi B.

In the semi darkness of her bedroom, Evi blinked and tried to focus on the alarm clock with the big, red numbers. 7:26. She raised her head, blinked again, checked for the light of day outside the drawn blinds. She always left a gap, never completely let them fall shut. She needed this confirmation. It made her get up in the morning.

It was winter, and at this time of day, it was dark like the deep of night.

Evi wriggled her feet clear of the sheets and sat up with her usual difficulty. She placed her naked feet on the cold ground, as firmly as she could. Then, slowly, she unfolded herself and stood.

For a moment, she waited till her bones had found their required positions within her body. She swayed but did not fall. She dreaded to fall: a broken bone at this time in her life would most certainly spell her end. She had seen it in others, had heard stories. If she fell and broke her bones, she would end up in a carehome, she would not be allowed to remain in her flat. Someone would come and take her away, and she would lose her freedom.

Evi made sure she stood solidly before she shuffled across to where her slippers were waiting.

Her granddaughter had asked once why she did not place her slippers so she could run her feet into them straight the very moment she got out of bed. Evi had shrugged but had not felt the young girl would understand her need for the contact with the hard concrete under the lino of her bedroom, would not understand the requirement of standing up on a surface that was solid and strong till her body had prepared itself upright after the long night.

In the glaring light of the bathroom, Evi stood at the mirror.

Most mornings she dreaded raising her eyes to her image, but this morning, she wanted to take it all in. She touched her bony fingers to her wrinkled face. She pulled a grimace and investigated the four remaining teeth in her mouth, the teeth that had remained when all others had to be pulled out. With her wispy, sparse hair sticking up in all directions, she looked like a witch.

In front of her mirror image, Evi cried and watched the tears run across the deep furrows of her face like water cutting a path through ancient rocks.

She used to be pretty. Her skin used to be flawless. Her hair used to be thick and heavy, falling in waves across her shoulders. Her teeth had brightened her smile, the smile that had made her so adorable and had touched the hearts of those she had thus favoured.

'Ugly witch!' She spat at the hag she saw.

'No wonder nobody ever comes and talks to you. Ugly witch!'

Then she realised that she used to be much taller and how she had shrivelled up in the past year especially, and she considered her entire appearance.

'Angry dwarf. Ugly witch!'

Because she had done it for as long as she could remember, she squeezed toothpaste onto her brush and began her day.

Evi's house stood in the middle of town, but her apartment was still and silent as if it was the last inhabited place on earth. Bulbs illuminated the dusty solitude, and she switched them off as she walked into the kitchen to get dressed.

She looked at the coffee machine and wondered if she really should be bothered to make her morning mug, but she also wondered what her alternative could be.

The thought of not eating or drinking any more, to hurry the end of her time along, flashed into her mind, but when her tummy rumbled demandingly, Evi reluctantly equipped the machine with filter, coffee and water and set it to work.

While the coffee was brewing, she walked the few steps to the front door where she picked up the morning's paper.

There was a time when she had wanted to lay the table for three, simply so that she would not feel so alone. One day she had done just that and had tried to imagine a conversation with friends who no longer breathed on this earth. The conversation had ended in tears – her tears – when she realised that she was going crazy. She had abandoned pretending and had sat looking into her garden instead. Had taken pleasure at the green grass in her backyard, and the few birds that came to pick at the crumbs she threw them every so often. There had been flowers, then, and the rose garden her Ferd had planted for her was beginning to bloom.

Now it was winter: there was nothing but a heavy, water-filled sky, dirt and mud. No precious flowers and no birds. The garden was as lifeless and dead as she wanted to be.

Evi's routine was always the same: get up, wash, dress, breakfast. She read the paper, but her eyesight was dwindling so she only read the headlines that not always made sense because at times, she misread. But Evi always worked her way through the names of the obituaries. People died that were far younger than herself, and she despaired. Had they forgotten to fetch her? Evi was keen to get back to the greenest meadow there was, so why were they not coming for her?

The older she got, the more often she thought about death. She dreamt, day and night, eyes open or shut, of what she had experienced when she was a younger woman. So much had happened since then, when she almost died: she had seen her children grow up, had held her Grandchildren and eventually her Great-grandchildren. She was proud of all of them. She had seen them all married and do well. They all had good heads, and most of them had studied. That is what she had dreamt for all of them.

She had seen her parents die, then her oldest son and remembered thinking that no mother should see her own precious child be laid to rest in a coffin. She had cried when her Ferd had breathed his last: she had held his hand at the hospital. It had been a while coming, but friends had said that with people so close as them, she would not be long in following. That was in 2001, and now they were in 2017 and she was 93 years old, and she was still here.

Evi had laid to rest one of her granddaughters who had taken her own life. She cried so hard that she thought there were no more tears, but there always were more. No matter how large an ocean she cried, there was always more inside of her.

Evi's life had been full to the brim, but she was sick of it. Sick of looking at herself in the mirror, seeing the deterioration, the effects of her own aging. None of the old ones that had come before her had mentioned about this aspect of their lives.

'Why?' she asked for the umpteenth time and got no answer.

Evi wished for an end and saw nothing. She listened intently but could not hear anybody coming to collect her, to tell her that she no longer needed to struggle, that now she had come to her deserving end.

With her hands in her lap, she sat and stared at the semidarkness outside her backdoor. The coffee machine sputtered, and she stood. Mechanically, she walked across, fetched out a mug, filled it with the hot brown liquid, then added milk and set the steaming drink on the kitchen table. Reluctantly, she bent to the fridge where she extracted butter and runny honey, before she stretched to fetch the loaf from the top shelf. Her hands knew how to use the slicer machine, circling once, twice, till a hefty slice of bread was cut. Grabbing her knife from the sink, she settled down for breakfast.

Before she guided the first bite of bread into her mouth, she remembered her medicines and stood once more. Her bones pained her, more than usual, and she was glad to sit back down and eat.

Afterwards, she spent almost an hour going through the paper. She looked, still only 9:25.

Evi huffed.

The day was not moving along: time like goo. She hated time. She hated death who had forgotten her.

Before she started on cooking her lunch, she noticed that the forecast for the night was a whopping -5C. She worried for her roses and considered wrapping them in sheets, but then decided against it. If they died, they died. As they should.

After lunch, Evi laid down on her settee. She wrapped in her blanket, closed her eyes tightly and waited for sleep to come. She could have sworn that she did not fall asleep, but when she checked the big clock on her table, she realised that it was almost 3:30 in the afternoon.

In her kitchen, she found a piece of cake that someone had brought her a couple of days before. Who was it? She remembered the woman but could not think of her name. Nice lady, who popped by every so often - one of the ladies from the JWs. Evi did not mind. Over the years, she had sat with plenty of them, listened to their monologues about God and Jesus. At least, it was something different. Not that she believed in that sort of thing, she knew so much better, but at least it was someone who came to talk to her.

The day had remained dark. Looking outside did do nothing for Evi. Her mood remained maudlin and dark. Like the angry grey sky.

She decided against dinner later on, watched the 7o'clock news on the telly, and then turned off the TV. She also switched off the lights and for a while sat in the darkness of her front room, watching for the lights of cars swooshing by in the silence that was hers since her hearing had as good as left her. At least she no longer heard the cajoling of the crooks outside, she thought, but would have loved to hear the laughter of children playing in the sunshine once more.

It was about 8:30 that night, when Evi took off her socks and in her bare feet stepped outside where the cold night air was so sharp it felt like needle pricks against the parched skin of her face.

Someone once had told her that freezing to death was not a bad death at all.

Slowly, she allowed herself to slide down against the outside wall of her home.

How long would it take? She was old, and weak. Evi hoped it would be over soon.

With legs stretched straight out in front, she looked at the star-lit sky. There were people all around her, and yet she was the loneliest of them all, she was sure of that.

After a while, she struggled up again. What if she froze to the wall? Then someone would have to come and use a hammer against the fabric of the house where she had lived the past 40 years of her life. Or they would pull her away, and her bones might come lose off her skin. These were pictures that Evi hated.

From her kitchen, she dragged out a chair and sat. This was by far more comfortable!

Should she have taken a sleeping pill? Would that have made the passing easier?

If she died of her own accord, would she still be allowed to go back to the greenest meadow of them all? She hoped so. But even if hell awaited her for punishment for this, Evi no longer wanted to live. This was no worse than hell could be.

She closed her eyes and contemplated all those that had passed on before her.

If she was lucky, she would soon be with her Ferd again, and see her son and her Granddaughter. There would be all her friends from long ago. Would she recognise them? Were they waiting for her?

With happy thoughts and just a little bit of excitement, Evi fell asleep on her kitchen chair, in her backyard, in a freezing cold wintery night.

A hard kick to the metal leg of her chair made Evi jerk bolt upright.

'What the hell do you think you are doing?'

The voice was rough, but familiar. Disoriented, Evi looked at where the face should have been. Heavy perfume cloyed at the back of her throat and she coughed.

'It's not your turn', he hissed.

Evi swallowed.

'Have you come for me?'

'Fuck no', he swore. 'If you do this now, I have no end of trouble. Remember that last time? I was their laughingstock for no end of time. Don't you dare do it again!'

'I don't want to wait no more', she simply acknowledged, and tears welled up.

With something akin to empathy, Death stretched out a hand. Softly, he pulled her up, and with one hand under her arm, the other dragging the chair, he guided her inside.

'Here, sit by the heater. You don't wanna catch your death of cold.' He giggled.

There was something familiar and Evi relaxed. It was good to have company, even strange company like this one. Anything was better than being alone.

They sat, Evi with her back to the heater, and Death with his elbows on the table, looking at her.

'Most people don't remain as relaxed at you when I swing by', he faked in a nonchalant accent.

'Most people probably don't wait for you as longingly as I do.'

He considered her, noted how she had changed. Saw the ravages of old age in her face, the wrinkles, the grey, the lack of teeth, and the sickness that was inside of her.

'Why?'

'Why what?'

'Why do you wait for me ... longingly? Aren't you afraid of me?'

Evi pulled up her shoulders, her hands in her lap, her face to the floor by his feet.

'Why should I be afraid? I know the meadow ...' she left the words hanging in the night air between them, like dust motes gliding in sunshine.

'Ah. That!'

They sat in silence. The clock ticked away, slowly, irrelevantly. The night stretched in front of them, patient, calm.

'Do you want to go to bed?'

Evi raised her eyes.

'I don't think I could sleep. Not now.'

'What do you want to do?'

'Are you going to stay?'

Now it was Death's turn to shrug.

'It was meant to be an easy night anyway. I am sure nobody would miss me if I gave them another day.'

'What about people that are in pain?'

Death considered the bother he would get in should Evi succeed with her suicide. It simply was not her time. Yet.

'Don't worry. I can stay with you.'

'Do you play cards?' Evi inquired after a while.

'Sure.'

'We could play a little while. They are in the other room ...' but before Evi could tell him where the sticky stack of cards was kept, he had already returned with them.

'I have been watching you through the years.'

With bony fingers, he shuffled and dealt.

They played through the night. They talked. They even joked. There was a companionship between them, like a long-standing friendship. He had watched her, he had said, and Evi believed him and understood that there was no real malice between them.

When finally, the sun rose, he stood and stretched.

'You have to go now?'

'Yes', he said. 'But if you like, I will be back later.'

'To play cards again?' Evi smiled.

Her strange visitor nodded.

'If you like.'

'When will you come for me?'

He looked out towards where the wintery garden lay frosted and glazed ahead of him.

'Tell you what. I come and play cards again. And one day, I will simply tell you to come with me. How's that?'

Evi smiled and in the flash of an instance, he was gone. The cards lay tidy in their box before her on the kitchen table. Slowly, her aching old bones complaining, Evi waddled to her bedroom where she lay down, covered herself with her blanket and tried to sleep.

Weird or not, there was a visitor: a visitor who played cards and gave her all his attention. What more could she ask for?

My Best Friend

I don't want to be here. I have no reason to be here.

It was not my fault, none of it. I find it difficult to argue with the logic of it all, and I don't know why I am being punished. It was not me.

How can I explain this to you?

Let me take you back.

I was maybe six or seven when I met Jamesy. A year older than myself, he was taller and ganglier than the other boys I knew. He had brown, curly hair sticking up unruly. His smile was radiant and special: I knew even then that Jamesy was handsome.

We started hanging out, and just fell into place next to each other. After school and homework, I would head out, unnoticed, before anybody could stop me. Across the backyard, down the lane and into the fields, I would soon enough find him. Or he would simply sidle up to me and we would walk, either in companionable silence or sharing the day's events in minute detail.

Jamesy did not go to school like me. His parents did not care for such things. It seemed to me that they did not care for a lot of things: he was hungry often and we shared chocolate bars, sandwiches and cartons of cocoa – whatever I could grab on my way out. Mind you, I never noticed then, it was just the way it was.

Most of the time, he was in worn jeans. Remember when a few years ago, all new jeans had to have holes across the knees? Jamesy had introduced this fashion years earlier: his knees, often grazed from a fall off a bike or a tree shone through the gash in his pants that his mother never managed to mend. His t-shirts were always slightly stained, never clean and crisp like mine.

Jamesy was always there for me. When I had a bad result in one of my tests, he dried my tears and whistled a happy song. When I got smacked by my dad for spilling a bottle of red wine on the white tablecloth, he hugged me close. We huddled till sundown that afternoon, high up on the tree he had shown me how to climb.

But then, one day he started talking about being bored. He knew so much, knew about the animals in the forest, the plants you could eat, the stars at night, and yet, he wanted to learn to read and write. I suggested to teach him, but he wanted to join me at class. My heart started thumping when he turned up the following Monday, his hair brushed and forced down with spittle, smiling shyly. He simply walked into the classroom and snug into the back bench, next to Fat Herman who did not seem to care and who took up most of the double space at the table. When I turned around and looked at him, Jamesy winked back at me.

During the break, he carried my bag to the new classroom, uncaring of the jeers of the other kids.

We took our sandwiches together, drank our juice, huddled under the big tree in the school yard. Jamesy and I were inseparable, and nobody could come near us.

Jamesy was always playing tricks. There was the water in Clever Eddie's school bag, spoiling his first class, special credit homework. And the rolls of slightly soiled toilet paper all across the teacher's lounge. I received some strange looks for that one, but Jamesy had left no evidence and nothing could be traced back to either of us.

When I got into a fight with Cindy about the colour of my skirt or something equally inconsequential now, but highly relevant then, Jamesy decided to play a trick on Cindy.

He glued her flute together. Problem was, he hid the paste in my school bag and when I was called to the headmaster, he simply disappeared. For the first time since we had met, he did not stand up for me.

And when I got a bad whooping at home over the damage to Cindy's flute, it was three days before Jamesy turned up again.

'Where have you been?' I asked, but he ignored me. Instead, he showed me a bird's nest with tiny blue eggs.

He did not go to school for a month or so, but eventually, his thirst for knowledge had him sneak back in. He clung to the back row, always at Fat Herman's side. Fat Herman smelled due to his weight and constant sweating, so the seat next to him was always available. I want to believe that Fat Herman enjoyed Jamesy being there. But Jamesy was my friend, never his. I don't know whether they ever even talked to each other.

I was twelve when we started to have Physics. Jamesy was my lab partner, together with Sabrina. We were the only team of three, but the teachers let it slide. They seemed to like having him around.

Sabrina was an interesting girl. She was the first of us who grew up and started to show. I asked Jamesy if he noticed and asked what he thought about Sabrina, but he just laughed.

'You are my girl, always have been, always will be', he hugged me as he said it.

It was in lab when Sabrina started talking about a boy, she was keen on. He was two years ahead of us, and just to get him interested, she had started using make-up. She was that kind of girl. And then she started telling me that I would never get a boy interested in me, that I was plain and always would be, and unless I started growing up, I would always remain a dumb child.

Jamesy really hated the way she talked. I did not see exactly what happened, but he snapped and held her hand into the flames of the Bunsen burner.

I was expelled over that. I had to change schools. I had to take the bus, no longer was able to walk. I got another spanking at home, and I was crying and crying, but they were right: Jamesy was my friend, and I should have stopped him.

The new school looked sad. I was sad. Till about a month after my start when the door opened and Jamesy sneaked in. My world changed, and I started to smile again. It was like before, just without Sabrina and the Bunsen burner.

When I was 15, I caught the eye of a boy in my class. When Jamesy noticed how things were going, he stopped coming.

'It's okay, sweetness', he consoled me. 'It really is okay. When you want to be friends again, just call out and I will find you.'

I did not see him again for a long time. My grades picked up, and there were no more incidents.

I grew up, had my first kiss, the first grope in the back of a car on the way to the movies. At 18, I finished school and started an apprenticeship at a bank. With time, I forgot about Jamesy.

But then I turned 25. Instead of flowers and pralines, my boyfriend of 7 years told me that he was tired of me and that he was leaving. He grabbed his things and moved out. My birthdays would never be the same! Instead of going to our favourite restaurant to celebrate, I called for take-out and opened a bottle of rum just on my own. I finished the bottle. I was finished with being 25. I hated it. I wished for being 26. Or better even, I wished for 30. Or

60 and early retirement, away from prying eyes and pitying stares.

Two days later, I was serving a particularly bothersome customer when out of the corner of my eye, I spotted someone I thought I recognised.

There stood a young man, grinning that grin, raising an eyebrow just like I remembered from when we were children.

Jamesy moved in with me the very same day. It took minutes before I had forgotten the previous seven years. How could I ever have lived without Jamesy?

He still was tall, lanky, his hair still unruly. His jeans now were no longer full of holes, and he no longer fell off his bike or down trees. He worked but took some time out just to spend longer hours with me. I guess his parents had left him some money when they died in a car crash a few years earlier. Never mind. He was by my side, 24/7, and I loved every minute of it.

A year later, for my 26th birthday, he insisted that I invited a few old friends from school.

'Isn't it time that we properly apologise to Sabrina and the others, for all the little tricks we played?'

The way he explained it all, it made perfect sense.

So, on the day, at 3pm exactly, a timid Sabrina was the first to ring my doorbell.

'I had to think about whether I should turn up or not', she admitted, looking at her hand. The scars were there and would never leave, a souvenir of Jamesy till the end.

She watched me; her eyes guarded.

I went to organise the table, made tea and coffee and was about to bring the cake to the dining room, when Jamesy came running to the kitchen.

He had the big cake knife in his hand, holding it up like a sword.

It dripped blood.

'She was saying such nasty, horrible things about you, I had to stop her!'

He flung the knife at me and ran out the back door.

Haltingly, I checked. Sabrina lay dead, covered in blood. The police later told me that she had been stabbed 72 times. Only my fingerprints were on the knife. They could find no trace of Jamesy anywhere in the apartment. Even his toothbrush had disappeared.

The evidence is all circumstantial. But I am here now, locked away.

They call this the closed psychiatric ward. I have to remain here. For now. I guess I have to wait till they start believing me about Jamesy.

It is a dim and horrible place, full of weird noises and smells. I have not smiled since I arrived.

But just now, out of the corner of my eye, I have noticed that in the common room, there is someone waiting for me. I am so glad that I have a friend like Jamesy.

The Man with the Wheelbarrow

I don't like the rain. Rain is not nice. Rain makes my hair wet and I don't like that. It feels like it rots my brain. It rains far too much.

It is even worse when it snows. When it snows, it is so cold that my beard gets stiff. One time, I snapped off a big chunk of it. I held it in my hand, a piece of wire wool, dirty grey. Almost took some skin with it. Really screwy. When it defrosted, it looked ... well, weird like. And my face hurt.

I don't like the sun. Sun makes my eyes cry. Makes me sweat as well. It used to bother me and I stank even to myself, but now ... that part of it does not matter that much anymore. Maybe I just got used to the stench.

When I was young, I liked the fog. There was a calm when you were enveloped inside that fog, like a blanket, so snuggly and comfortable. These days, it only ever gets really foggy down at the coast. I don't get there often enough.

I like it best when the weather is just weather. You know, just ... normal like. Weather where you can do what you want, not hampered by rain. Or snow. When the sun does not blind you and makes your eyes water. When you can just be. Yourself. I like that. Not too hot, not too cold, just right.

Weather is important to me. I spend all my time with it, in it, through it, so it must be. I wake up in the mornings, and I open my eyes and think, wonder what today brings ... I squint at the sky: I check for clouds; I check for sunshine. Tell-tale signs. Not that I have to worry about what to wear. It's not like there is much choice these days. When it rains, I don my mac – an old plastic thing that was bright red at some stage but is now simply pink and cracked. The colour. The coat itself is still okay. For now, it holds the water off me. Fingers crossed.

When I was younger, stuff was important to me. I used to have a lot. Stuff, that is. I had a house with a garden. I used to have a big black car. Vroom vroom, I used to shoot down the road. Mind you, I had to be up and about and go to work. Then. Rush rush rush, from here to there – so I could get more stuff. The house – it was full of stuff. I had a library full of books. An entire shelf with CDs and DVDs – I loved music. Now, I still love music, but I no longer need to listen to it loud. I playthings in my head. I sing along to my head-music. If I run out of words, I make them up. Sometimes, my new words are much better than the real ones, and I laugh. Laugh out loud. People look at me funny when I do that, but I no longer care.

When I had the house and the car, I also had a wife. A son. He was gorgeous, and really clever. He had just started school, when there was an accident. Don't remember the details, but one day he did not come back home. I got back from work, and my then-wife, she was crying. I no longer had a son after that.

 I missed him. She missed him more. And when she could no longer drag herself up in the mornings, she found a way to be with him. I remember her funeral: I don't remember that of my son. So long ago, what was his name? When I talk about him, I just call him Junior. It works and nobody listens anyway when I talk, so who cares? After her funeral, I tried to sell the house. I came home after that service, and I looked around and all that stuff, it did not do anything for me any longer. Nothing made sense anymore. I remember the emptiness and thought: 'What the heck?'

 I moved away. I changed jobs. I ended up in some grey, industrial town. It rained so much there! Or were they my tears? I don't remember. Don't care. Doesn't matter.

The flat I had ... it was okay. No longer with a library, but it had a comfy bed. They terminated me. They said, they could not have someone like me working for them. They said, they needed employees that came on time, every workday, that dressed properly and that ... washed. They were really fussy 'bout that. I wasn't. Not anymore.

I stayed in the apartment. I sat and watched out the window. Watched the rain. Watched as droplets fell on the windowsill, washed the bird shit off the glass, pooled in puddles on the walkways. When there was no more money, I left: Grabbed a suitcase, filled it with stuff and walked out. I took a train down to the beach. Not that I had money for a ticket, but nobody stopped me. Not getting on. And when the man came to check for my ticket, I pretended to sleep. Next, I knew, I woke up in a cell to sober up.

Someone stole my suitcase. It was blue, and it had wheels, so I did not have to carry things. Didn't matter. I didn't care. Nobody cared. I started to walk and kept on walking.

The sun was shining, and I ended up down at some park with the others who had nowhere to go. I looked at them, and they had the same eyes as me ... blinded by the sun. When you looked harder, you could see their emptiness. At a church, someone gave me new clothes when mine got too bad. You know, I was not looking after myself at all, and I stank. At my lowest, I soiled myself, I am not proud of that. I drank the cheapest booze I could lay my hands on – not always paid for, you understand, but it hit that spot, and served its purpose.

That time, I did not mind the weather. It could rain, it could freeze, and I was okay. I was drunk out of my skull; nothing came near me. In some ways, that was real happiness. That's what I thought: then.

All that changed when I found it.

I don't remember what made me walk into the woods that day. It was growing dark, and maybe I was looking for my wife and son, but I stumbled and fell. I knocked myself out. I slept. When I woke up, I thought I was sleeping in a proper bed, it was so soft. A bed that nature made. Couldn't smell it, not then. My nose, my taste buds ... by that stage, all gone. Could not remember where I was. Then I turned and knocked into something hard. A metallic clang. Didn't echo, was half covered in sodding pine needles and dirt. An upside-down wheelbarrow. Old, the wheel flat. I looked at it and saw myself.

On my knees, I used my hands to dig it up. Earth pushed under my nails, made my fingers bleed. There was nothing but silence. There was nothing but the woods, me and that horrible old thing, stuck in the dirt.

It was not pretty. It had dents and dimples. It was well used. But it worked. Like me.

There was nobody around – somebody had discarded this thing, like I had discarded myself. I took off my filthy coat and placed it inside the wheelbarrow. I pushed it along a path that did not exist, across the forest floor. It only took a short moment, and I started to sing. That was the first time I sang a happy song out loud, at the top of my voice. The first time since they had left me, my wife and son.

That wheelbarrow saved my life. I cleaned it. I went to a garage where I pumped up its tyre. The more I fussed about it, the more I myself got clean. My thoughts straightened. I no longer wanted to be with my wife and son.

Instead, I wanted to use this wheelbarrow. I wanted to bring it back to life. I wanted to live again.

 In a dumpster, I found basic gardening tools. A shovel with a broken handle. A rake with a few tongues missing. A two-pronged hoe. I loaded them into my wheelbarrow, covered them from the rain with a torn plastic sack, and started to push my load down the road. Whenever I ran across a garden that needed doing, I rang the doorbell and asked if I could help out. No money – maybe a sandwich, maybe a night or two in a garden shed. Maybe a bath.

At first, people were suspicious. I am not sure if I would have opened the door to myself, the way I looked! But I persisted. I had to look after my tools, I had to keep them busy and clean. I had a new purpose.

This was a few years ago now. I have a round I walk, all across the country, and even in winter I am busy as much

as possible. People know me. I am the man with the
wheelbarrow.

Pigeon Fancies

It was a nice spring morning when old Mrs K pulled up the blinds and got a surprise.

On the tiny bit of lawn that she called her backyard, there sat a skinny pidgeon. Not one of the usual kind: this visitor was light and brown with dark eyes that stared at old Mrs K and talked to her.

'Good morning', old Mrs K greeted the strange bird through the glass door.

The bird remained silent.

Nervously, it stepped sideways, left and right, waiting, staring at the old woman.

'Are you hungry?' old Mrs K asked.

The bird fluttered its wings but did not rise.

'I don't have anything for you. Let me look!'

Mrs K left the bird sitting on her lawn while she rummaged through her cupboards for some foodstuffs, she could feed the bird.

When she returned a while later, the pidgeon still sat where she had left it, dancing left to right. It did not even move when she opened the door with a noisy clang.

'Sorry', she said. 'I did not want to scare you.'

With her wrinkly fingers, she gently placed some seeds in a plastic dish and set it before the pidgeon.

'I have nothing else, but I hope you like this', she explained in her high-pitched old-ladies voice.

With delight, old Mrs K watched the bird pick at the seeds. She wondered at what it was doing in her yard, took in the white and brown markings on the bird's back, marvelled at the speed at which it picked at its food.

'O dear', she said. 'You must be hungry!'

When the dish was empty, the bird turned around, left a hefty dropping on the tired grass and flew off. Her hand shielding her failing eyes against the bright sun of spring, Mrs K followed the path of her visitor till it disappeared beyond the rooftops.

Later that day, she remembered to pick up a small pack of bird seeds, just in case her visitor returned.

The next day, old Mrs K was disappointed when she raised the blinds and there was no pidgeon waiting for her. Almost sad, she shrugged and followed her usual routines with just a trifle less enthusiasm. The bird had not talked back at her, but she had felt something different just by its presence. Late at night, tugged into bed, she wondered if she should get a bird for herself, but then rejected the idea: she was too old for the responsibility, and a caged bird was not a happy bird. She decided that she would put out more bird seeds in the hope of attracting more of the feathered visitors.

When old Mrs K pulled up the blinds on the third day, there sat the pidgeon waiting for her. She smiled, greeted the bird, and filled the plastic dish with two handfuls of seed for the bird to feed on.

As before, the bird looked at her full of interest, but did not fly away as she approached with the food. Calmly, the old lady talked to her visitor, asking about its family and why it was sitting in her backyard.

When the blinds on the first-floor apartment were drawn open, the pidgeon fluttered up but resettled instantly to pick some more on the seeds, like a little hammer, clack-clack-clacking away.

The window on the first floor was opened, and a young woman put out her head.

'Good morning, Mrs K!' she greeted.

'Good morning, Stella', the old lady called back without averting her eyes from the pidgeon.

'What a fanciful new friend you have', Stella called back.

The pidgeon scrambled into the plastic dish to be the easier able to get to the seeds. It did neither care nor worry about Stella.

'Yes', Mrs K mused. 'It is quite pretty.'

'And rather tame, don't you think? Where did it come from?'

Old Mrs K shrugged.

Stella, a steaming cup of tea in hand, still in her pyjamas and slippers, slowly moved down the outside stairs to stand next to Mrs K.

'Look', she whispered after taking a few sips of her brew. 'It has a ring!'

She pointed with her mug to the bird's leg where a yellow banding showed.

'This pidgin belongs to someone', she explained. 'I bet it got lost on its way home.'

Surprised, old Mrs K looked up.

'A homing pidgeon?'

'I guess that is what they are called. I mean, it does not look like the usual things that gawk across the square, right? They are all blue and grey and not like this, white and brown. This is a special bird.'

Unsure, old Mrs K looked at the bird that now was finishing the last of the seeds.

'It just appeared a couple of days ago.'

As on the last visit, the bird turned, pooped and flew off, its path followed by two sets of eyes.

'Leave it with me, Mrs K. I will find out.'

Old Mrs K picked up the empty dish to thoroughly clean it, careful to avoid the pidgeon turds, while Stella went back upstairs to change for work.

Stella was as good as her word. She googled about pidgeons, and found out from the local breeders' association that young homing pidgeons sometimes got lost on their first few flights; that they sat down to feed for two or three weeks, to regain strength, before flying off again and finishing their trip.

Because Stella liked old Mrs K, she went and bought a sack of special homing pidgeon food at the pet store and hauled it back to the house. In their lock-up at the side of the house, she filled a small bucket with seed for Mrs K to keep inside, while the remainder waited outside.

Mrs K was delighted but doubtful that the pidgeon would return.

In the next few days, a routine developed that pleased Mrs K tremendously. Every morning, when she raised the blinds, the pidgeon was waiting. Mrs K calmly spoke to the bird and felt its intent eyes on her face as if it was watching her, weighing her, about to speak and reply. On mornings when the rain was not pushing against the windowpanes, Mrs K left her backdoor open as she went about her household chores, every so often turning back to her visitor.

The bird remained for longer and longer stretches, often not leaving till lunchtime.

Old Mrs K told Stella that she would be glad if the bird flew away, home to wherever it had come from, once she had fed it for two or three weeks. In her heart, she prayed that the pidgeon would not leave. Ever. She enjoyed her mornings: whereas she had felt her age and had worked hard at getting up, now that she knew the pidgeon was waiting, getting out of bed was pure pleasure. It felt good to be needed, to shoulder the responsibility for another being.

Two weeks turned into three.

The bird showed no sign of leaving.

Instead, it would remain only for a short while in the mornings but returned at lunchtime.

Old Mrs K positioned her table settings so that she could watch the bird. This way, they ate together, and Mrs K felt less lonely.

One sunny afternoon, old Mrs K sat dozing when the pidgeon returned. Awakened by the bird's picking against the windowpane, the old woman looked straight at the pidgeon's face. For the first time, she noted that the feathers at its neck were turned up, making it look like it wore a collar around its head.

'You look like my Bertie with his crown of silver hair', she exclaimed. The pidgeon bobbed its head up and down as if in reply.

'Are you my Bertie?'

The pidgeon twisted and turned, its head picking at crumbs hidden in tufts of grass.

'I will call you Bertie. I hope you don't mind?'

Old Mrs K was happy thinking that her Bertie, who had passed too long ago, should be back to look after her. In her heart she felt that it must be close to her time. Had Bertie appeared to fetch her home? She sat motionless, smiling to herself, thinking of Bertie and their time together and that she really had had enough. Old Mrs K did not even notice that the bird flew off.

The next day, Bertie the pidgeon brought a friend along. Old Mrs K was surprised when she noticed a second bird next to Bertie.

This one was bigger, but of the market square variety in shades of blue and grey. Almost vulgarly, it pushed into the green plastic dish when she placed it outside for them, picked at the seeds at a much faster speed than her Bertie, and once finished, left a much bitter dropping right outside her back door. Before flying off, Bertie turned as if dancing, making sure she saw, coo'd and flapped away.

That afternoon, Stella from the first floor popped by.

'I see you now have two pigeons', she smiled.

'That second one, he just appeared with Bertie this morning.'

'Bertie? You named that pigeon?'

Old Mrs K shrugged.

'That collar of his, it reminds me so much of my Bertie. Here, look at his picture!'

From her lounge, she got a framed photo of her husband. Stella studied the smiling face, the kind eyes, and the shock of grey hair that ran like a crown at the back of the man's head. She had to admit, there was some semblance.

Stella nodded.

'Now I see. But you better be careful, or else you will feed all the pigeons!'

'O, don't worry: once that sack of feed you brought is empty, they will soon disappear!'

'So much for two to three weeks, right?'

They laughed.

'What does that pigeon breeder know about my Bertie, huh?'

After she assured herself that old Mrs K had all she needed, Stella made her goodbyes.

For a couple of weeks, old Mrs K fed her Bertie and that other bird. Both gained weight, both sat and waited for her at every opportunity: breakfast, lunch and dinner.

That insistence on regular mealtimes reminded old Mrs K of her cousin Peter who was big and brush, just like that second pigeon. Peter had been Bertie's friend, so she named her new visitor Peter.

When she told Stella, the young woman frowned. But she felt the joy with which Mrs K looked after these vile birds, she could not get herself to speak up. If this was the reason that old Mrs K smiled so much these days, then she should have her wish and keep feeding the birds. Instead of reprimanding old Mrs K, Stella went and bought a second sack of pigeon feed.

Not long after, two more pigeons appeared. After some consideration, old Mrs K named them Marnie and Peggy after her childhood friends who, like Bertie and Peter, had passed a long time ago.

Because Mrs K did not want to have all the birds from town on her small backlawn, she only fed them once Bertie was one of the kit.

She filled their green plastic dish, placed it so that she could see them, then sat in her chair by her table and smiled at the eager birds picking at the seeds, pushing each other in and out of their food.

One Saturday in October, Stella was late getting up. Lazily, she turned on the radio and to her surprise, the commentator mentioned their small town.

Stella did not catch the entire piece, but enough of it to be wide awake: that day, for no reason at all apparent to the radio station, all pigeons had disappeared from around town.

She stumbled and almost fell over some shoes and clothes that had been flung to the floor as she scrambled to pull open her bedroom blinds.

It was a scene from Birds, but even spookier since it happened to be for real: hundreds of pigeons sat, like sardines in their tins, pushed tightly into all flat spaces in the tiny patch of lawn old Mrs K called her backyard. Silent, they sat and waited for old Mrs K.

Unable to move, Stella stared.

The pigeons hardly moved; no sound made its way to Stella's apartment. They stared as one at old Mrs K's drawn blinds.

Old Mrs K opened her backdoor, brought out the green plastic dish, flung seeds over the flock of birds that she greeted one by one. From her window, Stella could see the smile on the old woman's face and in the glint of the sun, the tears that fell freely. Tears of happiness and calm.

Then, old Mrs K spread her arms wide and allowed the pigeons to settle on her sleeves, her shoulders, her hair, her hands.

Bertie, who perched high on old Mrs K's head, raised his beak to the heavens and let out a sound like a command and as one, the pigeons began to flap their wings. More and more came to hold on to old Mrs K, as her body slowly started to rise.

Hundreds of wings flapped as they bore the body of old Mrs K high above the rooftops, and home to heaven.

About the Author

Esther is an international woman. By day a Safety Manager, she spends her spare time writing novels, short stories, and now has started on poems. Originally from Germany, she has spent most of her life in the English-speaking world and writes in English in the first instance. Nowadays, she is also working on translations so that her writing can be found in both languages

Books By Esther Jacoby

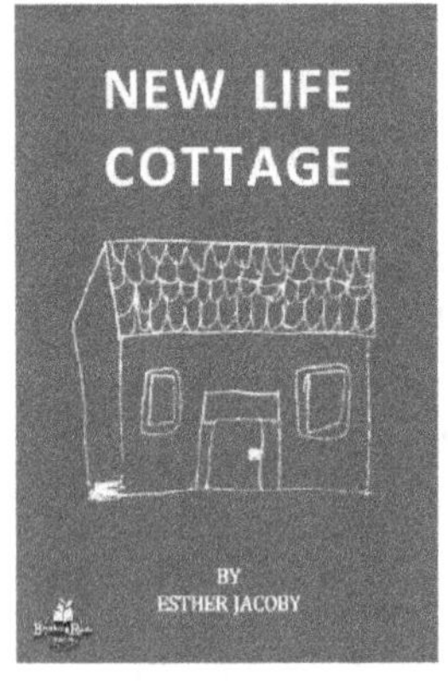

New Life Cottage

Friendship, Loyalty, Trust.

Hatred, Betrayal, Loss.

Three women find they have more in common than their friendship. Together, they embark on a journey that will stretch their faith in each other and in themselves.

Print ISBN: 978-91-986710-5-6

Ebook ISBN: 9781393669357